Your
Healing
Isn't
Linear

Written by Alessandra Brochu

How to Use This Book

In order to get the most out of this book, it is helpful to keep a pen or pencil handy for journaling prompts, exercises, and for your own reflections and self-love questions.

This book is meant to be written in, paused with, and returned to whenever you need it. There is no right or wrong pace to move through these pages. Take your time, skip around if you feel called to, and come back to sections as often as you'd like.

Some questions and exercises may bring up emotions or memories. Go gently with yourself and only do what feels supportive in each moment.

This is your space. Your journey. Your process.

For the girl I once was, for those before me and those who will come after me, and for everyone who is finding their way back to who they are.

Your journey begins here...

Healing chapters

Part I

Understanding the Patterns

Part II

When the Body Speaks

Part III
Reclaiming Yourself

Part IV
Self-love & Integration

My Beginning

I opened my eyes. Morning light crept in... Saturday morning, to be exact. I remember lying there, staring at the walls of my room, simply aware of being awake. Not a single coherent thought surfaced. My body functioned. I was breathing, my heart was beating, but my spirit felt absent, as if it had quietly slipped away in the night.

Nineteen years old, underweight, my face red and puffy, eczema flaring up across my skin. I felt nothing but a heavy sense of resentment toward life, toward myself, and toward the fact that I had made it through another night to face another day. Existing felt burdensome. Breathing itself was a struggle, as if some invisible weight had settled on my chest, pressing down with the weight of unresolved pain.

What would I be forced to endure today? What new stress would arise? What fresh lies would I be expected to navigate? How much more could I possibly take?

The truth is, I don't remember everything. My memories are fragmented. Scattered shards that emerge at unexpected moments. Now I understand that's how trauma works. It's the brain's way of protecting you through a process called dissociation.

It tucks away the worst of it deep in your subconscious so you can keep going. But some memories never really vanish.

They wait, quietly, ready to be triggered by the most innocuous things: a loud noise, the rumble of wheels on pavement, the specific way someone coughs.

I can walk into a restaurant a hundred times, and it's fine. But on the hundred-and-first, something as simple as the way a waitress hands me a menu can send me spiraling. In an instant, I'm no longer in that restaurant. I've been transported back to a place I fought so hard to escape. My body is present, but my mind is gone. I shut down. I can't speak. I can't think. I can't even breathe. Reality blurs, and for a terrifying moment, I lose myself entirely.

To someone who hasn't experienced this, it's almost impossible to explain. People often ask, "Why did you stay?" Or "Why didn't you just leave?" Or even worse, "I would never let that happen to me."

I used to say those same things before it happened to me. Before I understood how manipulation works. Before I realized how years of mental and emotional abuse chip away at your sense of self. Before I learned how gas-lighting, control, and lies can reshape who you are emotionally, mentally, and even physically.

It changes you. Sometimes so profoundly that one day you wake up and don't even recognize yourself. You're hollowed out, stripped of your essence, while the person who broke you moves on to their next victim.

I'm not writing this just for catharsis. I'm writing this in the hope that someone, somewhere, will read it and feel seen. That they'll realize they're not alone. They're not weak. They're not crazy. They're not to blame.

Healing isn't linear. It's messy, and painful, and unpredictable. But I hope this can be a starting point for someone else. A moment of clarity. A reminder that it does get better. That survival is strength. And that, together, through education, empathy, and honesty, we can break these cycles so they end with us.

PART I

Understanding the Patterns

———— * ————

You were not imagining it.

Chapter 1
What makes a "toxic" person

A toxic person is someone who's behaviors add negative experiences in your life whether that be emotionally, mentally, physically, etc. People who may be seen as toxic are in some cases going through really tough times in their lives and may act out in ways that are unlike themselves. Every human being is unique. Everyone has issues and their day to day problems. Toxic behaviors can also come from a fear based mentality such as fear of intimacy or fear of trust and openness to be their authentic selves.

Toxic relationships start and end every day. It would be a rare case if someone has not had an experience with someone who was labeled toxic at least once in their lives. When you think of someone who is "toxic" what traits come to mind?

1. Sarcastic
2. Passive aggressive
3. Flaky
4. Secretive

5. Cocky
6. Self centered
7. Irresponsible
8. Cold/insensitive

...The list goes on.

You may think of people in your life who have one or two of these traits, but when there's a list of them, you may start to notice that something isn't right.

Understanding when there is a toxic person in your life comes from, in my opinion, experience. You don't know when someone is bad for you if you've never experienced it before. It's even more difficult to spot when it is someone who raised you or has been a part of your life since you were young. This could be a mom, dad, aunt, grandfather, sibling, family friend, etc.

Once you've had your experience with toxic people, you start to become aware of what traits, patterns, and similar experiences to look out for in your future relationships. Knowing what a healthy relationship should look like in any of its forms is as imperative as knowing what a toxic person is. A healthy relationship on any scale should be 50% + 50%.

A give-and-take relationship that is equal and full of love, care, support, understanding, communication, forgiveness, acceptance, kindness, and appreciation for who you both are as human beings and as a whole. Some days a healthy relationship will even feel like 30% + 70% or 40% + 60%. Even so, it will still be healthy and equal in love and respect. A healthy relationship, whether it be romantic or platonic, needs to make you feel relaxed and at ease.

you

can

~~get~~ *grow*

through

this

The biggest misconception I learned to shy away from is the "butterflies" when you meet someone for the first time. Many people I've met, have misunderstood this for a long time! If you meet someone for the first time and they make you feel nervous, that is a normal human experience. If you like them or find them attractive, it happens to us all... However, if you continue to see this person and they make you feel sick, nauseous, tired, dizzy, worried, anxious, or otherwise, it is your body telling you something is wrong.

Your subconscious mind and your body can sometimes sense danger before you realize it's there. Think for a moment about when you've felt scared or been in a situation where you've run or reacted before understanding what was happening.

That's your body sensing danger and helping to keep you safe. For example, when I was younger, about fifteen years old, I walked into a store for my mother to buy something for her. She waited in the car, and I was walking down the aisles. A man was walking down the same aisle as me, and I automatically felt a difference in my body. My muscles tightened, my shoulders raised, my heart began to beat faster, and my palms turned sweaty. I told myself I was overreacting, but my body was telling me otherwise. The man proceeded to open his jacket and stuff items inside. He then began to yell at the clerk for the money in the register.

He was robbing the store. I calmly left, and we drove away. It took me about twenty minutes to process and understand what was happening. I told myself I was fine, but my body told me no, you are not fine, and you are not safe. What happened to my body also occurred with bad relationships, friendships, situations, and experiences throughout my life. The only difference with my experiences was that I didn't listen to my body, always dismissing it as "I'm overreacting; nothing is wrong."

Many times, when your body does this, it doesn't necessarily mean you're in physical danger. People who are not good for you mentally or emotionally can also cause this body reaction, or may leave you feeling tired, drained, with a headache, or sick after spending time with them.

For if one moment you feel that a relationship is a little "off," then it's time to break the relationship down and see if there are any positive points that matter to you within a healthy relationship that match your relationship with this person.

Being in any type of relationship should bring out certain feelings or sensations. Your physical body will react in different ways as well. Being around someone healthy for you will allow you to feel at ease, calm, and even energetic.

Self Love Questions

1. What toxic traits or experiences do you already know to look out for when you feel that someone might be toxic?

2. Do you feel that there could be more than one person you know who has had some type of toxic behavior?

   If so, what traits did they show you that made you stop and think?

Your physical body will be in a restful state, and you will feel like you can truly be yourself. Think for a moment about someone with whom you connect. How do they make you feel when you are by their side? Can you be your most authentic you?

Many factors can contribute to a person being toxic. Some toxic people have a root to their behaviors, as it may have stemmed from immaturity, negative patterns, fears, past traumas, high levels of stress, recent experiences, or their upbringing. For example, a toxic trait like emotional baiting, which is when a person intentionally makes you angry, annoyed, or sad, can stem from abandonment issues and neglect in their upbringing.

Needing constant reassurance from others, like compliments, awards, or feedback, can also come from abandonment issues and emotional neglect. Being cold or flaky may be caused by high levels of social anxiety or stress, while being sarcastic may be their way of regulating their emotions in stressful situations.

The traits are singular and have a root cause that can be amended with the right tools and mental/emotional help/support; yet, some traits are never addressed, and people begin to develop more traits or deepen the ones they have already had to make them a part of who they are.

Some toxic people stay toxic, and in their extremes, there may be more to these toxic people beneath the surface.

According to the World Health Organization (WHO), nearly one billion people worldwide, approximately one in eight individuals are living with a mental health disorder, making mental illness one of the leading causes of disability globally. Some mental illnesses hinder relationships, and they are often confused or go unnoticed. Psychopaths, narcissists, and sociopaths are commonly misdefined and flipped. To start on your journey of healing, it is important to understand the differences, as some toxic people may have multiple traits that can come from a mental disorder.

In this book, we will focus on the three main mental disorders that are most common in the mental health world. Psychopath, narcissist, and sociopath. These will be broken down so you can briefly understand their traits and understand how they may be tied to whom you are healing from. Throughout this book, there are self-love questions and other fill-ins, as you may have noticed, which I encourage you to use. Please write in this book. Really, using this book to your advantage is my hope, and that you take something from this to use on your healing journey.

The following descriptions are common patterns of traits rather than formal diagnoses, and individuals may display these characteristics to varying degrees.

A psychopath is often believed to be incapable of feeling emotion, but this isn't entirely accurate. Rather than lacking feelings altogether, they experience emotions in a very limited way. Over the years, a psychopath can learn to mimic feelings in social situations so well that you may never realize who you are dealing with unless you dig very, very deep. Even then, it can be difficult to truly know due to their chameleon-like disguises.

A narcissist is someone who is out for themselves. Narcissists have a "god" complex. They believe they are the best, and no one can ever measure up to them. Narcissists rarely apologize as they believe they are never at fault. In many cases, narcissists will devalue anyone around them to make themselves feel and seem superior. They are not afraid of stepping over others to get their way, and if they fail, it's definitely not by their own hand.

A sociopath is someone with a huge disregard for social norms and laws. They tend to break rules, stalk, steal, and have aggressive behaviors. Sociopaths also have difficulty controlling impulses, managing responsibilities like work or paying bills, and may have a disregard for their own personal safety. Think of someone who enjoys a life on the edge and doesn't seem to mind a broken bone or two for the sake of "fun."

Self Love Questions

1. What healthy traits (positive points) and experiences do you know to look out for or think you should look for when you feel someone might be the right fit for your life?

2. What do you wish to gain from this book?

3. How can you show yourself kindness and love today?

Chapter 2

Major traits of a psychopath
(toxic tendencies)

Listed are traits from the Hare psychology checklist. This checklist has the most common traits that a psychopath may have. The Hare psychology checklist is used by doctors and the police to diagnose and test. Of course, we are not all doctors, but common sense goes a long way.

  How this checklist works is that you must read the list and mark your person with either a 1 or 2, depending on the level of severity. As you may see, I added stars next to some on the list. These are of my situations and also some of the most popular traits that I will be going into detail with, so we can better understand them. Obviously, someone with no psychopathic traits would receive a score of 0. A score of 30 or more qualifies as someone to be a psychopath. All 40 points would be a prototypical psychopath. In my case, my person in mind received a score of 31. This checklist is a great tool to start your journey to better understanding and healing.

Keeping in mind your toxic and their tendencies, see if any of these traits make sense to your situation.

To transform

...we must first

practice patience
with ourselves ...

Hare psychology checklist

1. *Superficial charm

2. Exaggerated high sense of self

3. *Always in need of attention

4. *Pathological lying

5. *Cunning and manipulative

6. *Lack of remorse or guilt

7. *Shallow effect" fake emotional responses

8. *Lack of empathy

9. *Parasitic lifestyle

10. *Poor behavioral controls (violence)

11. *Sexual promiscuity

12. *Early behavioral problems

13. *Lack of realistic goals

14. *Impulsivity

15. *Irresponsibility

16. *Failure to accept responsibility & actions

17. *Short-term relationships

18. Juvenile delinquency

19. Criminal versatility

20. Revocation of conditional release

A psychopath is someone with these traits. They don't fully understand the damage they cause to others, not because they don't know what they're doing, but because they don't process empathy, guilt, or emotional consequences the same way. A psychopath's brain functions differently from that of a typical person. Many psychopaths show reduced activity or differences in areas like the prefrontal cortex, the front part of the brain near the forehead, which controls impulse control, decision-making, and emotional responses.

These differences aren't always caused by physical "damage." They can come from a mix of genetics, early childhood environment, trauma, neglect, or sometimes brain injury. Some psychopaths grow up in harsh or abusive environments, which can affect how the brain develops and how emotions are regulated. That said, when the prefrontal cortex isn't working the way it should, it can seriously affect behavior, decision-making, empathy, and guilt. In certain types of testing, this part of the brain doesn't respond the way it normally would when scenarios or questions require an emotional reaction.

For most people, when you run a red light, your brain kicks in immediately. "Will I get pulled over?" "What if I hurt someone?" Your heart may start racing. Your palms might sweat.

Those signals show up in brain scans. When someone with strong psychopathic traits is asked similar questions, those warning responses can be weak or not triggered at all.

What I would give to get a scan of my toxic brain. To actually see what I have had to figure out and teach myself all these years. I'm sure most of us would love that.

In some cases, people who have been exposed to long-term abuse or manipulation can begin to pick up certain behaviors. This does not mean you have become a psychopath. You are NOT a psychopath. The fact that you are reading this book to educate yourself, reflect, and rebuild already shows emotional awareness, motivation, and care. Those are things psychopaths do not operate from. Have you ever heard the saying, "People always want what they can't have"? People with toxic tendencies often gravitate toward those with the most strength, emotion, love, and empathy because these are traits they struggle to experience in themselves.

Remember: throughout this book, I've included self-love questions meant to help you pause and truly reflect. This book is here for healing and guidance, and I hope these questions help you dig deep, open yourself up, and begin a healthier season in your life.

Self Love Questions

1. What are your strengths?

2. How do you love yourself?

3. Is there something about yourself that you find unique?

There are many traits of a psychopath, as well as traits of a narcissist and sociopath. The most common traits of a psychopath that have been well documented, and some that I have personally had the pleasure of experiencing, are the ones that I will discuss in detail.

1. Superficial charm
2. Compulsive, pathological lying
3. Cunning, manipulative
4. Lack of empathy
5. Shallow affect (fake emotional responses)
6. Lack of realistic goals
7. Lack of remorse or guilt

Some of these may seem a little confusing, but when explained, we can make more sense of them all. If some of these traits do not relate to your person; feel free to skip to the sections that most resonate with your situation. Remember, coming out of a toxic relationship with someone does NOT mean they are automatically a psychopath, narcissist, or sociopath. There are a lot of factors within a toxic relationship, and this must be considered when starting your journey to discovery and self-love. Throughout the book, to keep an open mind to all situations, I will sometimes refer to people with these tendencies and all others as the "toxics."

1. Superficial charm

When you meet these people for the first time, it may seem like they have the world at their feet. They have the perfect personality. They have a lot of friends, and they know how to draw attention from a crowd. They may seem like a sculpted version of what a perfect person should be. Kind, sweet, caring; they have it all. Nothing seems to be wrong with them. This is normal. In my experience, this is a trait I've seen in many toxic people.

They have a way about them. It is behind closed doors that the "real" them comes out. This superficial charm also applies when you begin to date this person. They again seem like Mother Nature herself crafted them to your liking. They slowly get you to believe that you are #1. Destined to be together, the perfect fairy tale. I believe toxics do this as what I like to call the "mouse trap tactic." Think of it this way: There is a mouse around your house. You can't seem to catch it because it is too fast and smart for you. So every day you lay out a small piece of cheese. Days go by, and the mouse slowly gains your trust. Each day, the mouse comes closer to you.

Finally, the mouse trusts you enough to come right up to your hand. Finally, you can trap the mouse. The mouse started to trust you because you gave it exactly what it wanted. You gave it exactly what it needed to be happy. Your toxic first gave you everything you wanted to get you to a place where they wanted you to be. In love, devoted, loyal.

Once they had you where they wanted you to be, they trapped you. You are now stuck in a cage made from fake trust, fake love, and care.

Please look up the Pavlovian experiment to learn more about this conditioning tactic.

2. Compulsive, pathological lying

"That wasn't me." "I didn't do that." "They are crazy." "That didn't happen." "I wasn't there," etc., etc., etc. Toxics are notorious for lying. Not just your small white lie, no, these are everyday, every second, any topic kind of lies. Psychopaths, especially, may even enjoy lying. They don't just do it to save their asses; they generally enjoy the game of the lie.

How extreme this is depends on where your person falls on the spectrum. When it comes to psychopaths, some go as far as fully buying into their own lies. Imagine meeting someone for the first time. They ask you what you do for a living. In reality, you are a manager for a small company. (Beautiful job, nothing wrong with it!) Now, you are never going to see this person again, so you lie and set yourself up as the owner. You want to impress this person, and again, you are not going to see them ever again, so why not?

Everyone has told a little white lie before, but psychopaths do this on a whole other level. You know that in reality you are not the owner, but when a psychopath says that they are the owner, they ARE the owner.

When they say they're a well-known musician, have the president's cell number, or eat dinner with Oprah on the weekends, they can say it with so much confidence that it starts to feel real, even to them. They can carry on these lies for months and even years to everyone they know because it is real to them. After a period of time, it becomes real to everyone else as well. (Scary, right?)

When this comes down to the topic of you, having someone lie to you every day about everything CAN make you feel like you are, in fact, going a little crazy. Especially when you know they are lying, show the facts of their lie, and they still stand by their story as if it's true. For me, the lying game was constant. It was there all along, even in their youth. But I never truly saw the issue until I woke up that one day and decided that it would be the last day that I ever dealt with them again.

3. Cunning, manipulative

Although scientifically, psychopaths/toxics may have differences in brain function, this in no way, shape, or form hinders their ability to be perceptive. With everything I know now and have experienced, I can say that psychopaths and toxics are EXTREMELY strategic and calculating. They know just what to say and do to get what they want, and that includes you! They can make you jump through hoops for them if you aren't careful. They will turn you into their circus monkey for their amusement. They will befriend you if that means you can get them to where they want to go. They will also stomp you down for the same result. Manipulation is a big one. For me, it was the famous "silent treatment." I was already too far gone. We would argue almost every day. I would be deemed crazy and irrational.

By that time, I actually believed there was something wrong with me. When we argued, they would start their usual game. "Why do you always do this? Stop overreacting. I would never lie to you." Then, silence. This silence would last for days. The longest three weeks. By the 1st week, I grew paranoid. Thinking something had happened to them or that I was actually crazy.

Their family members would, of course, have no idea of what was going on because they would walk around telling everyone how happy we were. Yes, we were still dating, and NO, no one should ever do this to anyone. This creates unneeded stress that no one deserves. By the end of this silent treatment, they would text or call back as if we had never stopped talking.

When I mentioned to them why I was ignored for three weeks, they would have no idea about the situation, brush it off, laugh, and I would be crowned "crazy" once more.

4. Lack of empathy

What impacted me the most during my seven-year on-and-off relationship was the lack of empathy. There was emotion when it benefited them, but rarely when it mattered to me. This is often linked to differences in how a psychopath's or toxic person's brain functions, especially in areas like the prefrontal cortex. Empathy doesn't always register the same way.

According to LiveScience, people with milder psychopathic traits sometimes show emotional responses, but mainly when pain or consequences are directed at themselves. When that same pain is experienced by someone else, the brain response is often reduced or completely absent. In other words, empathy can be self-focused. In more extreme cases, empathy may be nearly nonexistent altogether.

This takes me back to countless memories when my toxic would show his true colors. I remember crying. They had already cheated on me multiple times. Texting exes, other girls, meeting them, etc. We were trying to bring our relationship back on good terms. But when they decided to flirt and get the waitress's' number in front of me, it all unfolded. The "I don't know what you are talking about." I was there when this happened. It happened in front of me. They know this, too. So there I was, shaking with anger, frustration, crying, falling apart. Them?

They smiled and started laughing. Leaning back against the car, arms crossed, laughing...LAUGHING. I can't describe the feeling unless you've been there or have experienced this before.

It is honestly too much. To watch someone who you believe is your future laugh at you while you cry. Enjoying your pain and taking it in like sunshine. This happened to me countless times. Another time was when I last saw them. It was New Year's Eve. Cheating again. I was in all ways done.

They had sucked the life out of me, and I had nothing left. I was storming to my car; they, of course, grabbed me and told me not to leave. They played the good partner and hugged me. I heard crying. In the twelve and a half years that I knew my toxic, they had never cried in front of me before. But I knew.

They begged me not to leave, and I pulled away from that hug because I knew. I heard crying/sobbing, but I knew there were no tears. I was right. No tears. I was furious. I even asked, "You aren't even crying; why are you faking it?" I got a big smile and laugh right in my face. I can't make this up. I wish I were. So, I got in my car and drove off. I never came back. I left that house empty, alone, underweight, anxiety written, and a stranger to my own self.

Everyone's story is different. What feels severe to one person may seem small to another. That's okay. Pain can't be measured or compared. And not everyone is capable of feeling love and empathy in the same way.

<u>5. Shallow effect</u>

This trait falls in line with my story about the lack of empathy. Shallow affect means that emotional responses, such as fear, anger, sadness, joy, disgust, trust, anticipation, or surprise, are limited, muted, or flat. For many toxic people, these emotions are not experienced or expressed in a typical way, and they often don't fully understand them. In some cases, even inappropriate reactions take place when others are suffering. My toxic would laugh when there was a death in the family or when a tragic event occurred. Instead of feeling sadness for loved ones or offering comfort, laughing and joking became their default response.

When someone is upset or sad, a psychopath or toxic person may recognize the emotion on a surface level but fail to emotionally connect to it. Because the emotion itself isn't genuinely felt or understood, these reactions can show up at the wrong time or in the wrong way, making their responses feel confusing, disturbing, or completely disconnected from the situation.

6. Lack of realistic goals

Do you have a goal in life? What is it? Everyone has a goal. Even if it is very small, you still have one. How about the future? You probably still have an idea. This is a trait that might resonate with most of you. Lack of realistic goals. That means either they do not have real long-term goals or their goals don't really make sense. For example, "I want to live in Antarctica, live in a hut, and join the circus." I'm serious; this is what happens. For me at least. If a psychopath or toxic has a "goal," it is an out-of-this-world, not going to happen goal. An unrealistic, impulsive, or constantly shifting goal.

Another trait to look out for is a lack of consistent jobs. This is a BIG one. Either you are paying for everything, or your toxic is changing jobs every three to four months. My situation was both. I was paying for everything while they jumped from job to job when they got bored. Toxics struggle to function in society without consistent new stimulation. Hence, the crazy life goals, job changes, and a wide range of friend choices.

This was the biggest trap I fell into. Believing all these crazy ideas in an act of love and paying for everything they needed. They had such a carefree way of living. They didn't seem to care what would happen in the future, where they would be in ten years, what they were doing next week, nothing.

That's why I think most people are drawn to these types of toxics. It's inviting being so "free." Most of us get sucked into this sense of freedom, and we become accustomed to the rose-colored glasses and forget the real picture of what's going on.

It's okay to dream, and it's okay to change jobs. But when it becomes a constant pattern, and they start living off other people's hard work, the glasses slowly come off.

7. Lack of remorse or guilt

The last and most common trait is a lack of remorse or guilt. This means they feel little to no genuine remorse for what they've done. They know that what they are doing is seen as wrong, but they do it anyway because of the lack of emotion that is normally associated with a "wrong action." My toxic told me he loved me and couldn't wait to see me after an event while texting another girl the same. On the same day, at the same time, while we were all in the same room, a row away from one another! Of course, it came to light, and they were confronted.

> "I don't know what you want me to do."
>
> ...they would say.

All the lies, cheating, and emotional beat-downs meant nothing to them. They continued to do this because any remorse they felt was shallow or didn't last. They wanted some action. Maybe they got bored. Maybe they wanted so badly to feel something that they used other people's pain as fuel. Using my love and care, and the love and care of other girls, just to try to feel something. My toxic continued to do this to more girls. There was no little voice inside my toxics head saying "STOP! THIS ISN'T RIGHT." This behavior continues because caring, guilt, and accountability don't register in a meaningful way.

BE
BOLD ENOUGH
TO LET GO
OF WHAT NO
LONGER
SERVES YOU

Chapter 3

Major traits of a narcissist
(toxic tendencies)

A narcissist, in a summed-up phrase, thinks they are "hot shit." They present themselves as if they are the best living thing to ever walk this planet. Narcissists often have a "God-like" complex and see themselves as above others. They want to be on top and are often focused on status, success, and how they are seen from the outside as the ones who have it all.

Narcissistic traits can develop from trauma, neglect, rejection, and/or a lack of emotional support in childhood.

They can also develop from an overly sheltered and overly indulgent upbringing, where everything is handed to them. Because of this, narcissism is better understood as a pattern of traits shaped by early life experiences while a psychopath is more closely linked to differences in brain function rather than being purely shaped by experience.

From *Psychology Today*, there is a checklist for narcissists. Listed are some traits that are mostly seen, but not all traits are listed. Unlike the Hare checklist, there is no numerical rating, but feel free to mark the ones that pertain to the person in mind if they match. As before, I've placed a star next to the most popular traits that we will be breaking down in detail.

1. *Is passive-aggressive
2. *Denies and dismisses others feelings (lack of empathy)
3. *Is a different person in public vs at home
4. Identifies as the victim
5. Turns your problems into their dramas
6. Is very critical or sarcastic
7. *Feels superior to others
8. Gaslights
9. *Avoids introspection and lacks self-awareness
10. *Needs constant reassurance
11. *Has an exaggerated sense of entitlement
12. Feels above the rules
13. *Uses guilt or shame to punish
14. *Focuses highly on appearances
15. *Hyper-vigilant
16. Is prone to paranoia or conspiracy theories
17 *Flatters other to win favor

Feel free to skip to the traits that pertain to your person in mind. Keep a pen handy to make notes, for release and the self-love questions.

1. Passive-aggressive

People with narcissistic traits often use passive-aggressive behavior, and at times outright aggression. This can come in the form of blaming, invalidating feelings, belittling, guilt-baiting, the silent treatment, or shaming someone to exaggerate their own importance or maintain control. For example, when you are looking for something around the house and ask for help, they may treat you like a child. They might use baby talk or make fun of you. I have seen this in action. The toxic said, "Um, are you stupid or something? How many times do I have to show you this? It's right here where it's always been," then proceeded to physically move their partner's head in the direction of some paper plates. This caused a scene and made their partner feel embarrassed and even made them believe that they were "stupid." This may seem like a small or unimportant incident, but it is impactful, no matter how small it appears.

This pattern can be used to slowly create emotional and psychological dependency as well. Over time, the narcissist uses these small experiences to make you feel, and eventually believe, that you are less than or that you always need the toxic person's help with anything and everything.

With constant occurrences like this, you may start to believe that you truly need them to function or that you cannot go about your day properly without them.

With this passive-aggressive pattern, it is also common for your toxic partner to invalidate your feelings. Invalidating feelings means that if you are expressing yourself and you feel sad or upset, they will tell you that you are not feeling those things or that you are lying. They may even begin to blame you for "ruining the day" or "causing a scene." Blaming is as simple as it sounds.

Everything is your fault, and they will make it your fault for things they do wrong, such as not following rules, not following social norms, or not following norms of business or job practices. If a narcissist is upset with you, wants to teach you a lesson, or wants to regain control, they will bring out the silent treatment. The silent treatment is self-explanatory, and we covered this with psychopaths. They will not speak to you for certain periods of time, and you won't know why or what you did. Usually, what happens is that they will wait for you to reach out.

When you reach out and they finally answer, they will act like nothing happened or will blame it on you for the time away from each other. This results in you either apologizing or starting an argument.

Either way, the narcissist benefits, because you reached out or started an argument which reinforced their sense of importance and control.

Guilt baiting is a big one. Some examples of guilt baiting are "You wouldn't be where you are without me," "Since you're too busy to see me, then I guess I'll be home all by myself," "Remember, I was there for you," and "You are nothing without me." These are all used to manipulate and to make you try harder to win their love, affection, and acceptance.

2. Lack of empathy

The lack of empathy is a core trait that we will see and review within this whole book. This trait is what gets to all of us. Lack of love, understanding, and care for others. Humans, by nature, are social beings, and all of us have an innate desire to love, be loved, and be understood, so it may be hard to understand how some people just don't have this in them. Unfortunately, this can be true in certain people. Narcissists often act as though their well-being and "feelings" are more important than yours, which leads them to dismiss your emotions and frame you as insensitive to their needs. Everything may be framed as your fault because of your perceived inattention to them. We know now that it is the other way around.

A lack of empathy may also be seen in social settings. This can show up as withholding money, communication, or affection, or using threats or pressure to get what they want. For example, in business or at work, they may charm their way up, take credit for others' work, spread rumors, or subtly threaten to complain or accuse in order to move up the social ladder.

Narcissists often seek emotional dependence from others. Money can be used with you or others to do this. Financial manipulation is used to keep people close and in constant need of your person in mind to function in life. If your person in mind says they must be aware of all financial choices, bills, and expenses, and is the only one who has and is allowed access to all accounts, then this could be a form of financial manipulation.

They could tell you there is no money left in the accounts when there is actually more than enough to sustain you both, or they may use loans, credit cards, and other profits, like business income or savings, for their own use without you knowing it. This lack of empathy and accountability allows a narcissist to brush off guilt and live life however they want, without considering the damage they cause. I've heard countless stories from victims about narcissists opening credit cards or creating accounts using their partner's personal information without their knowledge.

3. Different person in public vs. at home / 4. Feels superior to others

A narcissist's personality can change at home versus in public. Narcissists want to be seen as the best and are often portrayed by outsiders as caring, funny, high in social status, and well-rounded. At home, they can be the complete opposite. A narcissist may be cold, quick to switch emotions, and make you feel like you are always walking on eggshells. Just as we discussed with psychopaths, narcissists tend to have this pattern of a wolf in sheep's clothing. They want to be on top of any status or situation, so they will present a vision of perfection when needed. They may go out of their way to be courteous to others, but often only if they know they will need them for something in the future. They may also reprimand someone in public to build their own satisfaction of being the "boss," which is why some people see them as high on the social ladder.

Many narcissists are drawn to power, money, and social status, and some may climb these ladders quickly. This gives them the upper hand when they want to use someone or a specific situation to their advantage. As discussed in the points above, a narcissist feels superior to others. This means they want to be on top in all matters and believe they are always right. They will bring others down so they can climb higher for their own selfish worth.

5. Avoids introspection and lacks self-awareness

Narcissists avoid looking within themselves to see the issues they are causing and the damage they are inflicting on others. This reflects a lack of self-awareness and an unwillingness to fully see or acknowledge their behaviors and traits. Narcissists often act as if all is well and treat the harm they cause others as no big deal. They can avoid this to not feel vulnerable. Looking within can bring up unwanted emotions or past experiences they would rather not face. Their lack of empathy also plays a role here, as they don't take in or truly care about how others experience their behavior.

6. Needs constant reassurance

Narcissists are created through early stages of life and experiences. This shapes them to be who they are today. Either from a highly neglectful childhood or an overindulgent childhood. Both sides of the coin create these traits and cause a narcissist to need constant reassurance of who they are and what they are doing within their life. A life with constant praise and positive reactions to their behavior is needed so they can thrive. Awards, compliments, money, status, and other reassurances are just the things to boost a narcissist and keep them running smoothly.

They will seek these validations from all points in their life to feel that satisfaction. This is why these toxics are so welcoming and kind to others.

7. Has an exaggerated sense of entitlement

These toxics swim through life as if everyone owes them something. If a narcissist does something kind for you, believe that they will come back when they want something and use their kindness as a crutch. An example of this could be if they helped you with some money; they will come back asking you for double that amount or for something they need that doesn't equate to what they helped you with. They will also make sure to add in " but I helped you with..." and "I thought you would be there for me just as I was for you." This is to purposely trigger your guilt, in which you will help them.

If you give a narcissist money as a favor, you may never see it back. If they give you money, know you will have to pay it back and maybe with interest (whatever that "interest" may be). Favors and "gifts" are never done out of kindness but rather a you-owe-me gesture. They will do this for you if you have something they want or need.

8. Uses guilt or shame to punish

If a narcissist doesn't get their way, they will often use different ways to make you feel shameful and guilty. They will say things like, "It's your fault the day is ruined," or, "Our date was going so great, how could you mess it up?" Guilt-tripping can also show up as, "After all I have done for you, how could you not help me just this once?" Guilt builds when you are involved with a toxic like this. Playing the victim also feeds this shame and guilt, making you feel like you did something wrong. "After everything I've done for you, how could you hurt me like this?" Narcissists can withdraw emotional connection, physical intimacy, and contact to punish you and make you feel like you did something wrong. Over time, your self-awareness, self-esteem, and confidence can be worn down and you may become dependent on this toxic person for validation and control in all matters.

9. Focuses highly on appearances

Narcissists want to be seen as the best, especially when it comes to appearances. They often prioritize looking their best and having the best things. This can include putting on a full face of makeup, doing their hair, and dressing up just to go to the supermarket. It may not always be this exaggerated, but you get the idea. It could also look like hitting the gym every day for hours to look their best, buying the best clothes, and going to all the appointments for hair, nails, and other beauty-related shenanigans.They also tend to look for others who enhance their image. Narcissists like someone who is "well kept," someone who takes care of themselves, and someone they can use as arm candy.Their focus on appearance can help them get others to gravitate toward them in business, socially, and in relationships.

10. Hyper-vigilant

Narcissists often display a heightened awareness of anything that could threaten their ego. This is not toward physical danger, but toward how they are being perceived. This constantly involves looking for changes in behavior from others, socially or at work. If a boss changes their demeanor, or if coworkers begin acting in ways that suggest rejection or disapproval, it is quickly noticed.

This feels like an attack on their self-worth and is often interpreted as rejection. Rejection hits hard for a narcissist, even if they don't show it. They are often insecure within their relationships and are constantly looking for changes that could be seen as cheating or rejection. They can show high levels of jealousy and make frequent accusations, which can slowly lead to control over their partner. Having their partner rely on them and need them for emotional support feeds this dynamic.

This heightened awareness is often used to scan for rivals, higher-status individuals, or anyone receiving more praise or attention. This is seen as an attack on their ego and self-image, even when, in reality, it is not.

11. Flatters others to win favor

Flattering others is another main focus discussed in some previous points above. While flattery can be genuine in healthy situations, in this case it is usually not meant to be kind or caring, but to gain something in return. Whether it be gifts, kind words, gestures, or going "out of their way" for you or others, most likely a toxic person will want something in return for these flatteries. These behaviors are also used to appear likable and, in turn, help them get what they need to climb any ladder. Socially, in business, or romantically. They use this to gain the trust of others and can also use it to influence or control a person's actions, especially in romantic relationships or family dynamics. Flattery can also be used as a mirror technique.

Mirroring is giving praise and compliments to those they want something from in the future. For example, imagine a toxic person sees a highly successful business owner talking about their experiences. The narcissist may compliment them on their accomplishments and praise them for how amazing they are on their journey. The business owner then sees the toxic person as approachable, kind, and respectful because of this flattery. In reality, the narcissist is doing this because they know the business owner has something they need, or because they want to get close to them due to the desire to have what they have. Whether that is connections, status, or opportunities.

Self Love Questions

1. Have you ever ignored your own needs or boundaries to keep the peace with someone who makes everything about themselves?

Why did you feel the need to do this, and how did it affect you?

2. When someone disrespects your boundaries or dismisses your feelings, how do you typically respond?

How can you respond differently to protect your peace?

Chapter 4

Major traits of a Sociopath
(toxic tendencies)

Sociopaths are individuals who struggle with empathy, and this can make them seem cold or disconnected from others' feelings. They're often charming on the surface but have a deep disregard for other people's well-being and the rules of society. While each sociopath is unique, certain traits are common in how they interact with others. Here's a deeper look at some of these traits and how they show up in relationships.

1. Lack of Empathy
2. Manipulative Behavior
3. Impulsivity
4. Irresponsibility
5. Superficial Charm
6. Deceptiveness
7. Blaming Others
8. Chronic Lying
9. Disregard for Rules/laws

1. Lack of Empathy

One of the most defining features of a sociopath is their lack of empathy. They just don't connect with the emotions of others the way most people do. This doesn't mean they can't act like they care, but they don't feel it. When you're upset or hurt, a sociopath may brush off your feelings or even ignore them completely, leaving you feeling alone in the relationship. For example, if you've been emotionally vulnerable with them, and they don't acknowledge your feelings or even mock you for them, that's a classic sign. This can create a one-sided dynamic where your emotional needs are neglected, and you feel like you're giving more than you're receiving.

2. Manipulative Behavior

Sociopaths are incredibly skilled manipulators. They know how to play with emotions to get what they want. This might look like guilt-tripping, flattering, or twisting the truth to get you to do something. In relationships, this often shows up as them shifting blame onto you or making you feel like you're the one in the wrong. For example, if they're caught in a lie, they may turn it around and say, "I only lied because you were being too sensitive." This kind of manipulation keeps you on edge, always questioning your own feelings and judgment. This erodes self-confidence and can make you feel like you're never enough.

3. Impulsivity

Sociopaths tend to act on impulse, without considering how their actions will affect those around them. Whether it's a sudden, reckless decision, like buying something they can't afford, stealing, or an impulsive outburst, sociopaths often create chaos in their relationships. For instance, they might storm out of an important conversation because they can't handle confrontation or decide to take a risky job offer after quitting their previous one days before just to maybe quit this new job in a couple of weeks. These sudden, unpredictable behaviors can create emotional whiplash for their partners, leaving them feeling unsure about the future or even afraid of when the next impulsive decision might happen.

4. Irresponsibility

Irresponsibility is another trait that frequently shows up in sociopaths. They don't feel the weight of their obligations in the way others do. Whether it's forgetting to show up to a family gathering or neglecting financial responsibilities, they don't seem to care about the consequences of their actions. In relationships, this might look like them promising to be there for you emotionally but repeatedly failing to follow through. It could be something simple, like them saying they'll call at a certain time and not, or something bigger like not respecting boundaries you've set together.

5. Superficial Charm

Sociopaths are often extremely charming when you first meet them. They know exactly what to say to make you feel special, and they can easily win you over with their confidence and charisma. In the beginning of a relationship, a sociopath might tell you how perfect you are and how lucky they feel to have found someone like you. But once they've hooked you, their charm can quickly fade. They may start treating you with indifference, making you feel confused or even questioning what went wrong. This "bait and switch" is all part of their cycle, and it can make you emotionally drained.

6. Deceptiveness

Sociopaths lie often, and to them it usually feels natural and effortless. They can lie about big things, like cheating, or small things, like saying they were "working late" when they were actually somewhere else. But they don't just lie, they also twist stories or leave out important details to fit what benefits them in the moment. In relationships, this kind of behavior slowly creates confusion and makes you question what's real. You may find yourself replaying conversations in your head or doubting your own memory and judgment. This constant uncertainty can become emotionally exhausting and draining.

7. Blaming Others

A sociopath rarely takes responsibility for their actions. Instead, they tend to deflect blame onto others, even when it's clearly their fault. This can look like them blaming you for their poor decisions or accusing you of being overly sensitive or unreasonable. For instance, if they break a promise or lie, they might say, "Well, you didn't remind me about it!" or "If you weren't so demanding, I wouldn't have to lie to you." In relationships, this makes it difficult to ever have an honest conversation about issues, as they never admit fault. You may feel like you're always the problem, and they are always the victim.

8. Chronic Lying

This ties in with #6. Sociopaths often lie even when there's no reason to. These lies can be big or small, but they seem to lie because they enjoy controlling the situation. They may even lie about things that seem unnecessary, like pretending they've done something they haven't or making up stories about their past just as we explained in the traits of a psychopath. In relationships, chronic lying breeds a sense of distrust. It can make you second-guess everything they say, and you might feel like you're living in a constant state of doubt. This crumbles the foundation of any relationship because trust is essential for any healthy relationship.

<u>9. Disregard for Rules or Laws</u>

Sociopaths often show a disregard for rules, laws, or social conventions, especially when those rules do not benefit them. They might break the law, ignore boundaries, or act impulsively without caring about the consequences. In relationships, this could mean disrespecting boundaries that you've set together, like invading your personal space, stalking, being dishonest about their whereabouts, or violating agreements you've made. For example, if you ask them not to see someone from their past, a sociopath might ignore your request and go behind your back. This disregard for your boundaries and trust can make you feel disrespected and unsafe, and over time, it can erode the relationship.

Recognizing the Patterns

As you may have noticed, sociopaths, narcissists, and psychopaths all share some similar traits, which can make them difficult to distinguish from one another. All three are often characterized by a lack of empathy, manipulation, and self-centeredness, and they frequently display dishonesty and disregard for others' feelings. However, while a sociopath is more prone to impulsivity and erratic behavior, a narcissist is typically grandiose and focused on gaining admiration from others, often feeling entitled to special treatment.

However, while a sociopath is more prone to impulsivity and erratic behavior, a narcissist is typically grandiose and focused on gaining admiration from others, often feeling entitled to special treatment. Psychopaths, on the other hand, tend to be more calculated and often have severely limited emotional attachment, engaging in cold behavior for their own gain.

What makes them hard to tell apart is how much their behaviors overlap, especially when it comes to manipulating or deceiving others for personal benefit. They all struggle to form genuine emotional connections and may use people as tools to get ahead rather than forming healthy, mutual bonds.

In relationships, these traits can lead to toxic and emotionally draining dynamics where you feel manipulated, ignored, confused, or betrayed. This can chip away at your sense of self, your confidence, and your ability to trust your own instincts.

Recognizing these traits is the first step toward protecting yourself. Understanding these psychological patterns allows you to set boundaries, step away from harmful dynamics, and begin choosing relationships that feel safe, balanced, and respectful. This awareness is not about labeling others, it is about empowering yourself to break free from cycles that no longer serve you.

Self Love Questions

1. Which of all these toxic traits/behaviors affected you the most during your relationship?

2. How did this change you from the person you used to be to the person you are now?

3. Is there more than one person in your life that you believe could have some of these traits? Friend, co-worker, family?

Expressive exercise

Let out your emotions... If you are comfortable enough, write a letter to your toxic about how a trait has changed you.

Let all your emotions about your experiences pour onto paper. When you are done, safely light a candle and burn your letter. Take deep breaths as you do this.

While your letter burns, and you exhale, imagine all that negative energy from your experience release into the air and out of your body. * You may do this exercise for each trait that has affected you.*

Afterward, take a few moments to sit quietly and notice how your body feels. There is no right or wrong way to feel here. Simply acknowledge whatever comes up with kindness. If it feels supportive, place one hand on your heart and remind yourself that you are safe, you are healing, and you are allowed to let go.

PART II

When the Body Speaks

——— ✳ ———

What the mind survives, the body remembers.

Chapter 5

You are not going crazy

The main reason that I am writing this book is to help others like me who end up in this unfortunate situation. Whether it be from any toxic relationship to their extremes, a psychopathic, narcissistic, or sociopathic one.

My goal is to build a community of strong others who are aware, confident, and willing to keep this knowledge and awareness growing. Emotional and mental trauma can scar a lot longer than a bruise. Physical wounds heal over time, but mental wounds need constant care, dedication, and treatment. If not treated, these wounds can stream on into your life for years to come and then can be passed on to others like your friends, family, and maybe to future generations.

It is important that after reading this book, you keep pushing through. Seek counseling if you need it. Read twenty more books if you need it. Travel, paint, cook, do what makes YOU happy, and do things that will help your mental health. This is YOU we are talking about.

Every
moment is
a fresh
beginning.

The most important thing to know and understand is that you are NOT crazy. You did absolutely NOTHING wrong. You are a combination of everything beautiful. You were hurt by someone who could not see your value, worth, and love. Your emotions, your happiness, your drive are all valid. People want what they don't have. Sadly, when these people can't obtain what they lack, they can take it from someone else. You were the victim. Not them! You wanted someone who equaled your unique beauty, and you ended up with a wolf in a mask. You are stronger than you think. Allow yourself to push through. Open up to others, be free, and let go. Become new and you again.

Many toxics use certain cues or phrases that will make you double-check your own sanity. Don't forget to include the silent treatment, belittling, name-calling, and escalated outbursts. These phrases will be repeated in almost every argument. This repetition makes you "double-check" yourself. These are just some of the phrases that will shake up your mind into thinking you are actually crazy, not worthy, and/or possessive or obsessive.

These are purposely used for just that. People who are toxic like to target self-esteem. The goal is to make you feel bad about yourself so they can feel better about themselves in the end. This is all used as manipulation, and in turn, you overly try to be the best you can be for that person you love.

- "You're crazy"

- "You're overanalyzing (overthinking) this"

- "You're so jealous all the time"

- "You're so emotional/sensitive"

- "I've told you this so many times"

- "What are you talking about"

- "You're always causing problems"

- "I don't know what you want me to do"

- "Why are you so obsessed with me"

- "You're ------------" (stupid, dumb, immature, annoying, an idiot, etc)

- "Its always something with you"

- "Why can't you be like------------"

- "Your always such a disappointment"

- " You're so boring"

Be proud
of your
growth.

Know and understand that all this was and is not your fault. It's only what they wanted you to believe. You are not crazy for wanting to be loved by someone. You are not crazy for believing that someone you care for was able to give back to you what you deserved. Nor are you dumb, stupid, annoying, possessive, and/or obsessive for seeing past their games and finding their blueprints to their schemes. You are extremely brave to climb out of this and move forward. You are so strong for wanting better. It is time to cocoon yourself in the love you deserve and focus on self-care, positivity, happiness, and your new healthy future. It is time to grow and open your wings.

So, how can you do this? How can you heal? Making time and space for yourself is best. Finding your worth and understanding how important and unique you are is essential. Figuring out what is best for you and seeing what you want to do first for YOU is important. For every person, this will look different. Maybe it's starting with self-care, or maybe for someone else it's journaling or opening up to a friend. Whatever you feel is best for you, begin with that. Make a list of things you want to do as well as who you want to be as your healing journey grows.

Be selfish
Do you

Self Love Questions

1. What phrases did you resonate with and what other things has someone said to you to make you feel "less than" ?

2. What tactics can you think were used on you to make you feel unworthy?

3. How can you be the change for yourself regarding your healing? What is your goal?

Chapter 6
Understanding your worth

Part of understanding your worth is recognizing how you ended up in your situation. The way to conquer and win this fight is <u>through</u>, so let's get therapeutic and dig into your past. As children, you are sponges, and anything that you see, hear, taste, smell, and touch affects you to some extent and creates building blocks for your road ahead. The people that help to shape your life are... you guessed it, your parents/guardians. Your caretakers create the foundation in which you grow and see the world.

If your parents/guardians tell you that grass is blue since infancy, you will believe it. If they feed you chicken nuggets and mac and cheese from the time you grow teeth until you start elementary school, believe me, that it may be difficult for you to try broccoli or carrots during school lunch. The same goes for the way your parents/guardians act around you, treat you, and speak to you. These actions shape your world for better or worse and do have long-lasting impacts all the way to adulthood.

Many parents/guardians did try their best, and with what we know now compared to thirty+ years ago about discipline, positive reinforcement, expressing emotions, and gentle parenting, I know that many parents/guardians did the best they could with the information they had at that time.

Yet, there are some parents who, because of their own upbringing, may have carried down some not-so-healthy habits that may have trickled down to you.

There are some of you who have had the unfortunate turn of experiences with abuse. There are some types of abuse that could have a long-lasting effect on who you are today.

- Emotional/verbal abuse: such as name-calling, shaming, belittling, yelling, scaring, taunting, being made fun of, blaming, threatening, withholding love or affection, etc.

- Physical abuse: such as hitting, excessive spanking, pushing, shoving, pulling, etc.

- Neglect: such as a non-present parent or not having the proper care for basic needs. Food, water, shelter, clothing, education, etc.

- Sexual abuse: includes inappropriate acts, groping, sharing explicit content, etc.

Self Love Questions

1. Was there a parent/guardian figure that you think could have caused a negative impact on who you are today?

2. Was there a trace of abuse in your childhood? If so, which kinds?

3. What blocks were handed to you as a child that you definitely need to replace?

These types of abuse, if any, that pertain to you could have had a negative impact on your upbringing. There are some other factors to take into consideration as well; maybe your parents/guardians were not around as often due to work to teach you the skills you needed, or you never had a certain parent figure to begin with. Other big factors could be a divorce, family split-up, immigration, death in the family, alcoholism, homelessness, or drugs. Who you are today is because of all these little blocks that were handed to you when you were young. Figuring out which blocks are falling apart and need to be replaced is our job in this chapter.

It could be a hard truth to face. The realization that a toxic person could actually be someone in your family. Your mom, dad, siblings, grandparents? Yes, this could be tricky. In some cultures, family is the basis and foundation for your lives. It doesn't matter how someone treats you or others because "they are your family." I always tread this area carefully because it could be difficult to completely cut off your father, mother, or someone who helped raise you. I understand. This is where your boundaries and personal opinions and beliefs come in.

As we get older, we see our parent figures act, talk, and be a certain way. Sometimes, it is all we know. Because of this, we begin to accept that other people are supposed to be this certain way because of what we are used to seeing when growing up. If you had a mother or father who disregarded your emotions when it came to getting hurt, being angry, or sad. Subconsciously, you may find partners or friends that do the same. Maybe you grew up in a home or with people around you that always had a temper. Anger outbursts, screaming, and maybe physical/verbal abuse. You may then have met many people now with these same traits. This is okay and understandable since this is all you knew.

Waking up as you are now and seeing that some people are not for you, a cycle needs to stop and a change needs to be made means you are on the right path to healing. Reframing your mind and releasing habits that may have been placed since childhood is sometimes no easy feat.

It takes dedication and drive, and constant compassion for yourself to redirect your mind to new and positive patterns. Healing isn't linear, and giving yourself the space to accept that some days will be easier than others will give you more space for healing and more time to have your new blocks settle in for your road ahead.

As my healing progressed, I realized that even though I went through a lot during my youth. Homelessness, parental divorce, emotional abuse, and neglect...I am responsible for my own happiness.

It was a hard pill to swallow, but understanding this opened my eyes to see and acknowledge that the relationships that I found myself in were because of this... It was all I knew, and I felt that because I was treated this way as a child, it must be the way I should be treated now.

Some can fully cut off a parent, guardian, or family member, and some may have to "tolerate" them in everyday life or at family functions. Respecting yourself, knowing what you will tolerate or not, could be helpful here. I made a list of things I would not tolerate from certain family members. Belittling, talking down, sarcasm. When these things happen, I distance myself with a boundry or confront them directly. I wasn't able to do this until I understood my power and how much control I had over my life, my experiences, and my choices.

Who I had to keep an eye out for because their traits didn't align with what I believed healthy qualities should look like in a person came with knowledge, time, and patience with myself.

Learning these and making my list served as a guideline for me to choose the right people I wanted to be close to in my life as an adult. This also helps when meeting new people.

There are certain signs to watch out for when meeting someone for the first time to know whether they are healthy to be around or on the more toxic side. Trusting your instincts is #1 in my toolkit, but it does take time to realize if you are not in tune with yourself and your body. Having that innate feeling of "this doesn't feel right" is your body's way of letting you know that this person is not the one to be around. When you feel like you have to be someone else around a person, lie about who you are to try to fit in, or walk on eggshells, then there's something definitely wrong.

Another thing to look out for is if this person is in a self-centered mindset. If they like talking about themselves and only about themselves. If they aren't asking about you or fitting you into the conversation, then that's a big red flag. Shaming you for your interests and/or making fun of who you are, what you like, and what you do is another sign of an unhealthy match, whether it be friends, family, or a significant other.

Finding someone open about your interests, kind, who can hold a mutual conversation, lets you express yourself, and is there for you in your best interest is something to look for.

If you are in tune with yourself, you can feel this in your body. When you meet someone healthy, you will notice a lightness in the air. Your shoulders will not be tense, your jaw will be unclenched, and you won't have any uneasy feelings in your nervous system telling you that something is off.

Think for a moment about an imaginary someone that you know that you will get along with. What traits about their personality do you like? Are they attentive? Do you feel safe? Does conversation flow effortlessly? Next time you are with anyone, notice your body and think about what you feel.

Understanding your worth can be difficult if you are just getting started on your journey of healing or if you never understood your worth. What does it mean to understand your worth? It means that you must believe wholeheartedly that you are deserving of all love and affection. That you are deserving of a happy life, wonderful friends, an amazing partner, a fulfilling job, and all that you have dreamed up for your life. Understanding your worth can be as simple as choosing you every single day you wake up on this planet. Choosing what makes you happy and what feels right to you and only you. Understanding your worth means that no one is in control of your life but yourself, and you have the power to make changes/choices big and small your way.

Chapter 7
Childhood trauma
Anxiety & PTSD

If you feel you were in a toxic family system from a young age, this could have caused you to develop some not-so-healthy habits.

What is anxiety?

Anxiety is something all of us have felt at least once. The overwhelming nervousness before a performance or staying up late at night, unable to sleep because of constant thoughts, is a common experience. Anxiety = stress. Small stressors in everyday life are normal, as healthy stress can help us grow and face challenges. Healthy stress can prepare us for upcoming events, give us warnings if we may be in danger, and help us respond when needed. An example of healthy stress could be you wide awake on Christmas Eve. Thinking of Santa and all your presents. Or the day before an exciting vacation. Yet, when it turns into constant everyday stressors, overthinking, fidgeting, etc., this is where it can be called anxiety.

When it overtakes your life and influences most, if not all, of your choices, actions, and emotions, then this would be seen as chronic anxiety. The World Health Organization, in a study, said that 300 million people globally suffer from anxiety, and only about 4% have spoken about this to a health professional.

Anxiety can come in forms of coping strategies that you may have developed to help you "relax" or to self sooth during a situation or experience such as...

1. Skin picking/nail biting
2. Hair pulling
3. Excessive scratching
4. Shaking/tapping
5. Rocking
6. Twitching
7. Cracking fingers consistently
8. Chewing on objects (always in need of oral fixations)
9. Constantly changing your mind or being indecisive
10. Canceling plans
11. "Ghosting" disappearing from friends and family (Not responding to calls or messages)
12. Overthinking (What if) mindset

These are only some common ones out of a plethora of habits.

Know that high levels of stress, prolonged anxiety and chronic anxiety, can also lead to other mental health conditions like depression, chronic fatigue, a lowered immune system, inflamed gut health, and even brain fog. Your body is deeply connected, and stress affects the body way more than you may realize.

What is PTSD?

Many believe that PTSD only comes from very traumatic events, such as war or sexual/physical abuse. In fact, PTSD, or Post-Traumatic Stress Disorder, is different for everyone and can even develop in someone who has come from a different type of toxic relationship or family dynamic. Homelessness, emotional abuse, and verbal abuse are the ones I've seen go the most unnoticed for PTSD.

As a child, being exposed to this has lasting impacts and can even affect the brain. Being exposed to an unstable family dynamic can contribute to PTSD symptoms or anxiety symptoms in children. It can then form into adult habits and chronic health conditions.

PTSD is the mind and body's response to overwhelming stress that the nervous system never got the chance to process.

It happens when something painful or frightening leaves a lasting imprint on the brain and body. When the body still feels unsafe even after the danger is gone. It's not only about what happened, but how it *stayed* within you.
These experiences can shape the way we see ourselves. It's not weakness; it's a learned form of protection. PTSD and trauma is not only flashbacks or nightmares. Sometimes they look like always needing control, avoiding closeness, or feeling numb when you should feel joy.

A dysfunctional family, emotional neglect or psychological manipulation, Being constantly criticized, gaslit, or invalidated or experiencing housing insecurity or homelessness can develop traits of PTSD and can show up as...

1. Intrusive thoughts & memories
- Constant replaying of arguments, hurtful things said, or traumatic events
- Flashbacks or emotional reliving of past situations
- Nightmares (not always graphic and can be emotional)

2. Avoidance

- Avoiding certain people, places, or topics that remind you of home/family/an experience
- Shutting down emotionally or avoiding relationships altogether
- Feeling numb or disconnected from your past/present

3. Negative changes in thoughts & mood

- Chronic low self-worth ("I'm not good enough," "Everything is my fault")
- Difficulty trusting others
- Deep shame or guilt, even when you didn't do anything wrong
- Persistent sadness, hopelessness, or emotional numbness
- Feeling like you're permanently "damaged" or "broken"

4. Hyper-arousal / Hyper-vigilance

- Constantly on edge, jumpy, or scanning for danger even in safe environments
- Difficulty relaxing or sleeping
- Angry outbursts or being easily irritated
- Startle easily or feel overwhelmed by noise, chaos, or conflict

PTSD Habits from Emotional Abuse or Dysfunctional Homes

Fawning
- Over-apologizing
- People-pleasing
- Trying to be "invisible" to avoid conflict

Dissociation
- Zoning out
- Forgetting chunks of time
- Feeling detached from your body

Inner Critic
- Harsh self-talk that mirrors how you were spoken to at home

Learned helplessness or self sabotage
- Feeling like there's no point in trying to improve your situation

Emotional flashbacks
- Sudden waves of shame/fear
- hopelessness without a clear trigger

PTSD Habits Homelessness or Housing Insecurity

- Fear of losing stability even when housed
- Hoarding or clinging to items as survival behaviors
- Difficulty trusting people or accepting help
- Anxiety about safety, abandonment, or basic needs
- Deep-rooted insecurity about being "a burden" or "not enough."

* You don't need to have had physical abuse to develop PTSD from emotional abuse or a toxic home.

* Childhood trauma or neglect often has long-lasting effects, especially if it was ongoing.

* Homelessness (especially in youth or after escaping abuse) can itself be traumatic and lead to PTSD even if no "violent" event occurred.

Think of anxiety as the future and PTSD as the past.

Anxiety creates overthinking of what if's, fear based thinking, and worry of what might go wrong in the future, while PTSD is focused on what has already happened in the past that may trigger you in the present.

A common result-
Abandonment wounds

Abandonment wounds form when love feels uncertain or unsafe. When the people meant to protect us and love us were inconsistent, emotionally distant, or left us feeling unseen. Even without someone physically leaving, emotional disconnection can leave deep marks that follow us into adulthood. When anxiety or PTSD is present, these wounds can resurface easily. The body stays alert, expecting rejection or loss. For some, this turns into clinginess. Needing reassurance, overthinking, or holding on tightly out of fear of being left. For others, it becomes avoidance, ghosting, pushing people away, or shutting down emotionally to protect themselves from getting hurt again.

Both patterns come from the same root: a deep fear of being abandoned. Healing begins by recognizing these reactions not as flaws, but as old survival responses. It's about slowly learning that you are safe now, that love doesn't have to hurt, and that you no longer need to leave yourself behind to feel secure. Healing begins when we start to recognize these patterns not as who we are, but as what we've adapted to survive. Recovery takes time, patience, and compassion for the parts of yourself that learned how to cope. It's about gently teaching your body and mind that you are safe now. That you can rest. That you don't have to live in survival mode anymore.

Self Love Questions

1. List 5 traits you know you do NOT want to see in any of your relationships.

2. List 5 traits you know you DO want to see in any of your relationships.

Seek within...
The answers
are there.

Chapter 8

The Nervous system
From stress to release

Your body is nothing short of a miracle. It's made up of over
30 trillion cells, more than 650 muscles, around 100,000 miles
of blood vessels, and a brain with approximately 86 billion
neurons firing in constant conversation. Each moment,
thousands of biological systems operate like a dance. Molecules
colliding, oxygen moving from your lungs to your bloodstream,
muscles contracting and releasing, tissues regenerating, organs
communicating with one another, and electrical impulses zipping
across your nervous system at speeds of up to 250 miles per hour.
Your heart beats about 100,000 times per day, your lungs take
in roughly 20,000 breaths, and your brain processes millions of
bits of information, even while you sleep. All of this happens
without your conscious effort even while you're simply sitting still,
scrolling your phone, or worrying about what's next.

Take a deep breath in right now...

Every single breath you take activates multiple systems. Oxygen travels from your lungs into your bloodstream, where it is carried by red blood cells to nourish your brain, your heart, your muscles. Simultaneously, carbon dioxide is removed from your body.

Your muscles, bones, skin, and organs are all working together with electrical signals and chemical reactions to keep you alive, alert, and balanced.

Most of us take this for granted. We wake up, scroll through social media, rush to work, think about bills, worry about relationships, wonder what the next hour holds, and rarely stop to notice how tirelessly our bodies are working to support us.

But knowing all that your body is doing and knowing that it is functioning for your greatest good, imagine now what happens when you add high stress to the equation. Imagine the toll that pressure, anxiety, or emotional overload takes on a system already operating at full capacity.

How Stress Hijacks the System

Stress is not just an emotional state; it's a full-body biological response. When you're under stress, especially over time, your brain shifts into survival mode. It activates the fight/flight/freeze system, flooding your body with stress hormones like cortisol and adrenaline. These are useful in short bursts; they help you escape danger, sharpen your senses, and react quickly. But in everyday life, the danger isn't usually a tiger. It's an email. A deadline. A breakup, or being late. A trauma you're still carrying. And those hormones don't know the difference. When cortisol is high for too long, it begins to wreak havoc...

What Stress Does to the Brain:

- It shrinks the prefrontal cortex, the part responsible for logical thinking, focus, and decision-making.

- It enlarges the amygdala, your fear center, making you more sensitive to threats and more reactive.

- It disrupts the hippocampus, interfering with memory and emotional regulation.

- It increases the risk of anxiety, depression, and PTSD, especially if left unaddressed.

What Stress Does to the Body:

- It suppresses the immune system, making you more likely to get sick and slower to heal.

- It raises your blood pressure and heart rate, increasing the long-term risk of cardiovascular problems.

- It interferes with digestion, causing stomach pain, bloating, and disorders like IBS.

- It leads to muscle tension, often in the neck, back, and jaw, causing chronic pain.

- It disrupts hormonal balance, affecting sleep, appetite, sexual function, and mood.

- Stress changes how you breathe, how your heart beats, how your blood flows, how your muscles hold tension, and even how your cells divide. It is not just "in your head"; it lives in your entire body.

Your fight, flight, freeze response

There are moments when your body reacts before you understand why. A tight chest, quickened breath, or sudden stillness: the body speaking in its own language of protection.

Deep within your brain lives the amygdala, your inner alarm system. Its job is to keep you safe. When it senses something that feels threatening, like a harsh word, a painful memory, or a moment of uncertainty, it sounds the alarm. In an instant, your whole body prepares to survive.

Fight

When your body believes strength is needed. You feel heat, tension, or a rush of energy that pushes you to protect yourself. It can look like anger, defensiveness, or a strong need to be heard. Beneath it all is your body saying,

"I'm scared, and I don't want to be hurt again."

Flight

When your body has the urge to escape. This can be to walk away, distract yourself, or stay busy enough not to feel. It's your system searching for safety through distance, whispering,

"If I can get away, I'll be okay."

Freeze

This comes when neither fighting nor fleeing feels possible. The body shuts down to protect you from overwhelm. You may feel numb, disconnected, or unable to respond. It's not failure. it's actually,

"I'll stay still until it's safe again."

These responses are not weaknesses. They are ancient, intelligent patterns designed to protect you. But sometimes the alarm keeps ringing long after the danger has passed. This is a way your anxiety, or your PTSD can show up in your body.

Healing begins when you start to notice your reactions instead of judging them. When you can pause, breathe, and name what's happening.

Step 1- You create space for choice:

"I feel myself tightening; I want to run; I feel frozen."

Step 2- In that space, you remind your body that it's safe to slow down, to breathe, to rest.

Step 3- You begin to rebuild trust with yourself:

"I can feel this, and I'm still safe."

That's where healing starts ... not by silencing the alarm, but by learning how to listen to it with compassion and showing it love in return.

How to calm the nervous system

Calming your nervous system does NOT happen overnight. It could take months or years, and for some, longer to have your body back to a relaxed and healthy state. It takes more than trying yoga for a day and saying namaste to your friends. It takes hard-rooted work and, as some like to call it, "shadow work" to really dig in and pull out the stressors that may have been in your body and mind for decades.

Creating a safe space and eliminating the stressors in your life, as well as practicing softer approaches to experiences, a healthier lifestyle, healthy relationships, boundaries, and communication, are all needed to begin this. If your body has been disregulated for a while, then it will be difficult to train your brain and body to a calmer state.

Notice what I said... difficult... NOT impossible.

YOUR

Nervous System

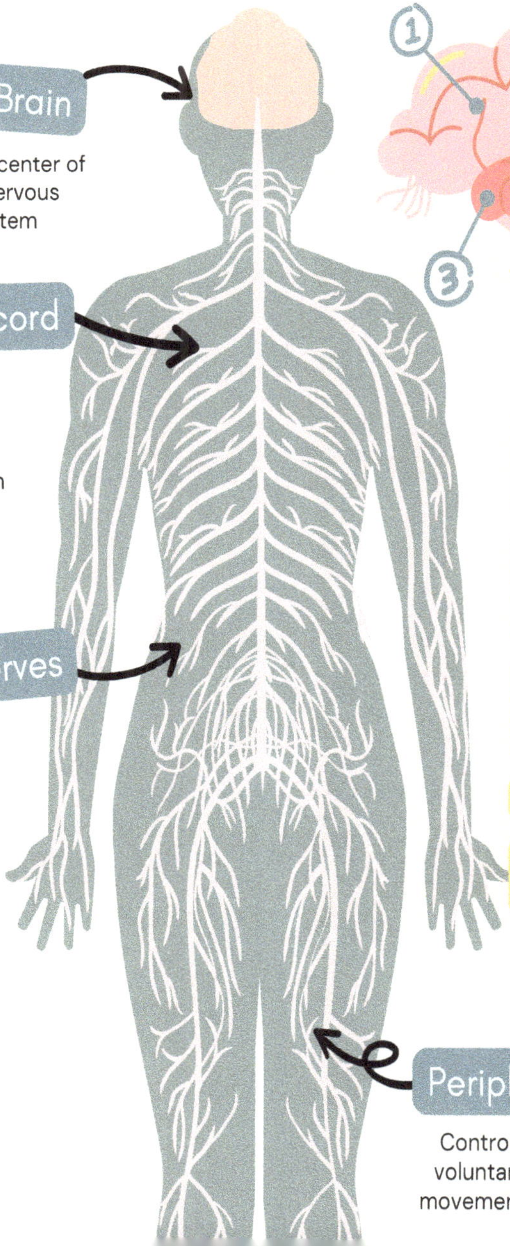

Brain

Control center of the nervous system

Spinal cord

A bundle of nerves that relay messages between the brain and the neural pathway

tonomic nerves

Regulates involuntary body processes such as digestion and heart rate

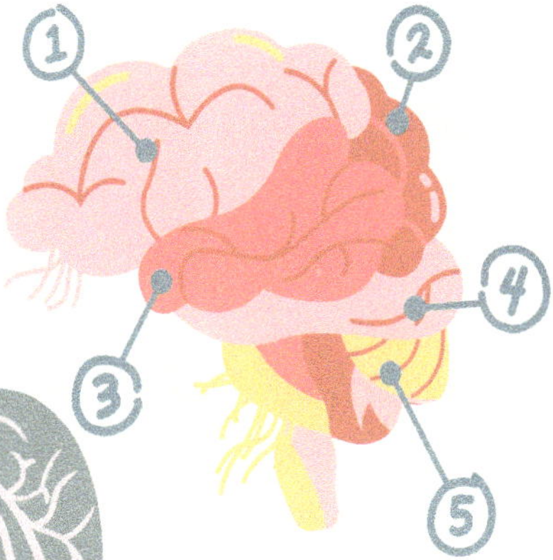

1) Frontal lobe: speech, motor control, cognitive skills

2) Parietal lobe: touch, pressure, taste, spatial awareness

3) Temporal lobe: hearing, facial recognition, processing memory

4) Occipital lobe: vision

5) Cerebellum: coordination, balance

Peripheral nerves

Controls our senses and voluntary actions such as movement and coordination

I won't lie by saying I am fully healed from my traumas and anxieties. They show up from time to time. Not feeling adequate with money or "wasting" food could trigger anxiety and stress in my body. Having to see certain family members instantly triggers my body to begin its fight/flight/freeze response. Thinking someone is upset with me or disappointed in me also triggers this response.

The difference now versus the past is that I am aware of my triggers, I know that communication is needed when this happens, and I know that my deep breathing, getting outside in nature, laughing, connecting with myself and understanding my journey, drinking water... all this helps, and I've noticed such a change in the strength I have to stop my fight/flight/freeze responses early on and tell my body and mind that I AM OKAY.

Trusting my body and myself, giving it love when this happens, not fighting it or pushing it away. Welcoming it with a warm hug, showing up with love and patience, and watching the trigger response melt away.

This is retraining your mind, your heart, and your nervous system to default. Training yourself to understand that there is no danger, no alarm, and that you are okay.

Make your own
"Calming my nervous system"
Diagram

Everyone is different. What helped me may not help you, and maybe the ways you calm your body and mind are based on your likes and interests. The next page is a blank diagram in which you can add your own ways to calm your nervous system.

This will be useful on your journey as you learn to navigate your authentic self and start to find those healthy relationships that we all seek.

In the diagram, you can add anything you would like that you may find helpful for your nervous system.

I recommend some physical, mental, and emotional ideas, as well as spiritual ones if you like that idea, to add to your diagram. The first diagram is just a simple example of how this could look.
*Rip your diagram page out (I won't get mad, I promise) and keep it somewhere you feel that it would be a great reminder for you when you need to calm your nervous system down.

HOW TO CALM YOUR NERVOUS SYSTEM

Eats foods that fuel your body & mind

Educate yourself

Find a passion

Surround yourself with good company

Treat yourself with kindness

SELF

Move your body

Limit screen time

Sleep, rest, SLEEP!

Everything you write down can be a guidebook for yourself in the future about what to look for when meeting someone new or trying to figure out who the right people are to have in your life.

Choose people who lift you up. Everyone will have faults. No human is perfect, but the people you choose to have in your life should be a reflection of all things positive and peaceful.

HOW TO CALM MY NERVOUS SYSTEM

SELF

Big journeys

begin with small

steps.

Part III

Reclaiming Yourself

———— ✳ ————

You were never lost. Only becoming.

Chapter 9

Attachment/Relationship styles

Your relationship style is how you function within a relationship (attachment style). Discovering where you are in your attachment style offers a glimpse into how you react to certain relationships based on your upbringing and experiences. This is a reminder again that everyone is different. It is okay if you have a style that someone else may not have. Your relationship style is impacted by your childhood, communication patterns, and experiences throughout your life. There are four that may give you a deeper insight into where you lie.

1. Secure attachment style

2. Anxious attachment style

3. Avoidant attachment style

4. Fearful-Avoidant (Disorganized) attachment style

Be gentle with yourself as you read through the attachment styles. Be open and accepting if you have an attachment style that may not be positive. To grow and heal is to have open arms for the parts of yourself that may not be pretty.

1. Secure Attachment Style

Characteristics: People with a secure attachment style are comfortable with intimacy and independence. They have a healthy balance of being able to trust their partner while maintaining their own sense of identity and personal space.

Strengths: Open communication, emotional support, trust, and stability. They're generally able to handle conflict in a healthy way and value emotional closeness.

By standards, a- Healthy 50-50 relationship

2. Anxious Attachment Style

Characteristics: People with an anxious attachment style often worry about their partner's love and attention. They may crave closeness and reassurance and fear abandonment, which can sometimes lead to clinginess or over-dependence.

Strengths: Passionate and highly invested in relationships, often sensitive to their partner's needs.

Challenges: Struggles with insecurity, jealousy, or emotional dependence. They may overanalyze their partner's behavior and feel anxious about their relationships, especially if they feel they are being neglected.

3. Avoidant Attachment Style

Characteristics: Those with an avoidant attachment style tend to value independence over intimacy. They might suppress their emotions and resist closeness, often distancing themselves from partners when things get too intimate or emotionally intense.

Strengths: Self-sufficient and autonomous, they are able to handle challenges independently.

Challenges: Difficulty with emotional closeness, vulnerability, and trust. They may seem emotionally distant or unwilling to open up, which can create tension in many relationships.

4. Fearful-Avoidant (Disorganized) Attachment Style

Characteristics: This is a mix of both anxious and avoidant traits. People with this attachment style desire intimacy but fear it at the same time, often leading to a push-pull dynamic where they jump between seeking closeness and pushing away.

Strengths: Can be deeply passionate and caring, but this often comes with confusion or inner conflict about their emotions.

Challenges: They may struggle with trust, commitment, and emotional stability, often resulting in relationships that have high inconsistency.

Self Love Questions

1. What relationship/attachment styles do you feel you currently have?

2. Do you believe these styles are something you would like to work on?

How They Relate to Real-Life Relationships:

In real-life relationships, most people don't fall into just one category but may move between styles or show traits from more than one. It is okay if you feel you relate to different attachment styles. This often depends on your past experiences, your current relationships, and where you are in your healing journey. For example, a generally secure person may sometimes act anxious or avoidant after repeated hurt, betrayal, or emotional inconsistency. An anxious person may work toward becoming more secure when they are in a stable, supportive relationship that provides reassurance and emotional safety. Likewise, someone with avoidant tendencies may slowly open up when they feel respected, not pressured, and emotionally understood. These shifts don't mean you are "regressing" or "failing," but rather responding to your environment.

It's also important to note that attachment styles are fluid. They can change over time, especially with self-awareness, therapy, healthy relationships, and inner work. Becoming aware of your attachment patterns allows you to pause, respond differently, and choose relationships that support your emotional well-being instead of repeating familiar cycles. Healing doesn't mean becoming perfect; it means becoming more aware of your needs, boundaries, and emotional responses.

How can I grow in my Attachment Styles?

There are ways you can change your relationship style through healing, trust, communication, and believing in yourself that you deserve a healthy relationship in whatever form. We will go through the different ways we can achieve this for each style.

1. Secure Attachment Evolution:

Growth: A person with a secure attachment style already has a strong foundation of emotional balance, trust, and healthy communication. However, they can continue to grow by learning to deepen emotional intimacy, support their partner in new ways, and adapt to changing relationship dynamics.

Challenges: The challenge for secure individuals is not necessarily emotional stability, but how to support a partner who may be struggling with an insecure attachment style without losing their own balance.

Tips for growth:
- Continually nurture trust by being open, honest, and consistent.
- Work on communication to make sure both partners feel heard and valued.
- Self-reflection is key to growth!

2. Anxious Attachment Evolution:

Growth: People with an anxious attachment style often find themselves in relationships where they need constant reassurance, which can lead to insecurity or over-dependency. Over time, they can learn to manage their anxiety and develop a more secure approach to relationships.

Challenges: Anxious individuals often get overwhelmed by feelings of uncertainty, leading to excessive clinginess or frustration when things don't seem "perfect."

Tips for growth:
- Develop self-soothing techniques like mindfulness, journaling, or meditation to reduce anxiety in moments of doubt.
- Increase self-worth by focusing on personal growth and hobbies, helping to lessen dependency on a partner for validation.
- Communicate needs clearly and recognize when they may be becoming overly needy. Learning to ask for reassurance without demanding it.

3. Avoidant Attachment Evolution:

Growth: Avoidant individuals often push people away when things get too close. Overcoming this involves learning to lean into emotional intimacy and trust without fearing the loss of independence.

Challenges: The primary challenge for avoidants is their discomfort with emotional vulnerability. They may fear being overwhelmed by their partner's needs or losing their own identity.

Tips for growth:
- Learn to open up; even small expressions of vulnerability (e.g., sharing a fear or a need) can make a huge difference in growing closer to a partner.
- Practice emotional check-ins with your partner, even when things feel uncomfortable. Start with small, manageable conversations about feelings and needs.
- Set boundaries, but in a way that still allows for emotional closeness. Be clear about your need for space while also being open to emotional connection.

4. Fearful-Avoidant Attachment Evolution:

Growth: People with this attachment style often experience a confusing mix of craving intimacy and fearing it. The key to growth is learning to trust oneself and one's partner while acknowledging and processing past hurts or traumas.

Challenges: This attachment style can lead to emotional whiplash, where they might desperately crave love but then sabotage it due to a fear of rejection or vulnerability.

Tips for growth:
- Acknowledge your fears. Understanding where they come from (often past traumas) can help reduce their control over your relationships.
- Seek therapy or counseling. Working with a professional can be crucial for managing both anxiety and avoidant tendencies, especially when trust issues are involved.
- Practice self-compassion. Learning that it's okay to have flaws or fears but still be deserving of love can gradually shift the fear-based responses.
- Communicate with your partner instead of shutting down; work together to understand your fears and find ways to navigate them as a team.

If you begin or currently have a relationship with someone who has a different relationship/attachment style, there are ways for you both to grow together and acknowledge where you each are on your journeys.

Healing isn't linear, so there is always room for growth and love.

Navigating Relationships with Different Attachment Styles:

When different attachment styles come into play in a relationship, it can create both challenges and opportunities for growth. These are some examples of the most common dynamics. Here are ways you both can help each other.

1. Secure + Anxious styles:

Challenges: The anxious person may need more reassurance than the secure partner is used to offering. The secure person, however, may then sometimes feel overwhelmed by the anxious person's emotional intensity.

This could show up as...
Secure partner: "I care about you, and I'm not going anywhere."
Anxious partner: "Are you sure you really mean that? How do I know you won't leave?"

Tips for Success:
- The secure person can offer calm, consistent reassurance but also gently encourages the anxious partner to self-soothe and build emotional resilience.
- The anxious person can work on building confidence/ manage anxiety through personal development.

- Communication is key: The secure person should be patient and avoid pulling away during moments of anxiety.

2. Secure + Avoidant styles:

Challenges: The avoidant might resist emotional closeness, which can create frustration for the secure partner who seeks a deeper connection and communication.

This could should up as...
Secure partner : "I'm here if you want to talk about what's bothering you."
Avoidant partner: "It's fine; I'd rather handle it on my own."

Tips for Success:
- The secure person can gently encourage the avoidant to share their feelings without pushing too hard, respecting their need for space but also encouraging connection.
- The avoidant can work on opening up gradually, recognizing that emotional closeness doesn't mean losing independence.
- Set clear boundaries and understand that emotional closeness may need to happen at the avoidant's pace, but it's important not to completely avoid intimacy.

3. Anxious + Avoidant styles:

Challenges: This is often called the "push-pull" dynamic, where the anxious person craves closeness, while the avoidant person pulls away when things get too intense. This can lead to frustration, confusion, and emotional instability for both.

This could show up as...
Anxious partner: "Can we talk about what's going on between us?"
Avoidant partner: "Why do we have to analyze everything? Can't we just drop it?"

Tips for Success:
- The anxious person should work on managing their neediness and practicing self-soothing techniques so that they don't overwhelm the avoidant partner.
- The avoidant person needs to recognize that emotional intimacy is essential for the relationship to grow and can try to open up more, even if it feels uncomfortable at first.
- It's important for both of you to have open, non-judgmental conversations about your needs and fears to break the cycle of tension.

4. Fearful-Avoidant + Any Style:

Challenges: Fearful-avoidants can create a roller coaster of emotional highs and lows due to their push-pull dynamic, which can be draining, regardless of whether they're secure, anxious, or avoidant. This, unfortunately, may turn into a toxic situation in which it may be best to distance yourself from this and reevaluate your relationship.

This could show up as...

Fearful-avoidant partner: "Part of me really wants to open up and trust you, but as soon as I feel vulnerable, I panic and push you away because I'm afraid you'll leave or hurt me first."

Fearful-avoidant partner: "I crave closeness and reassurance, but when you get too close, I feel overwhelmed and start pulling back, even though deep down I don't want to lose you."

Tips for Success:

- The fearful-avoidant partner needs to actively work on their trust issues and recognize their internal conflicts. Therapy or self-help work can be very important here.
- Their partner needs to be patient, offering support without enabling unhealthy behaviors, like avoiding tough conversations or shutting down.
- Communication needs to be honest and consistent, with both partners making an effort to meet in the middle.

Communication
Communication
Communication

There's a moment in my favorite movie, *Pride and Prejudice* (2005), when Elizabeth is at the piano and Mr. Darcy approaches her, clearly struggling to make conversation. He stumbles over his words before finally admitting that he finds it difficult to talk and open up to people. Elizabeth smiles and tells him he ought to practice. The scene always makes me laugh, but she's right. Communication isn't just about saying the right words; it's about showing up, listening, and learning how to connect. We all need practice, patience, and a little courage to truly reach others. When we give ourselves this, others can then reach us.

Taking accountability and knowing you can use some practice is amazing, and starting isn't as difficult as you think. Even if you are in the process of healing, taking a few seconds to let someone know you aren't available to talk or that you will reach out to them later is easy, fast, and shows respect for the other person(s) involved. When making plans, instead of disappearing beforehand, just let them know you can't make it. You can even go as deep as letting them know what you are healing from and allowing you some patience. Those who truly value you will be more than accepting with this and will be there to support you.

I've noticed that in almost every relationship, whether romantic or platonic, the root of most arguments, misunderstandings, separations, and trust issues comes down to communication and openness. Vulnerability, just like communication, is a skill that takes practice. When you show up for yourself and commit to practicing, you create space to find the people with whom you can truly be yourself, building the trust, safety, and comfort we all deeply crave.

Opening up to people you trust

Start gradually:
Share low-stakes personal details first, like a favorite hobby, a small accomplishment, or a funny story from your day.

Example: "I finally tried baking bread this week, completely burned the first loaf, but the second was amazing!"

Use "I" statements:
Focus on your own feelings and experiences rather than generalizing.

Example: "I felt nervous starting that new class, but it ended up being really fun."

Invite reciprocity:
After sharing, ask a related question to encourage conversation.

Example: "Have you ever tried something new that made you nervous?"

Take small steps to feel comfortable

Practice talking to yourself in front of a mirror or journaling thoughts before sharing.

Remind yourself that it's okay to pause or stumble. Feeling this vulnerability is normal.

Choose trusted people first, like friends or family who have shown support and understanding.

Check in regularly:
Frequent, short conversations build familiarity and comfort.

Example: Send a quick message or ask about someone's day, even if it's just for a few minutes.

Observe reactions and reflect:
Notice how the other person responds and how it makes you feel. Positive responses reinforce safety and trust.

Example: "They listened and shared something back. I felt more connected than I expected."

Celebrate small successes:
Recognize moments when you've opened up, no matter how small.

Example: "I shared a personal story today, and they responded kindly. Next time will feel easier."

Changing your attachment style or improving your relationship with someone who has a different attachment style requires a lot of patience, self-awareness, and communication on BOTH parts. If one person is trying their best while the other is idle, it will be difficult to change or improve your styles. As well as to have a stable and healthy relationship dynamic.

For growth to happen, it will take intentional effort from BOTH people involved. What I love about attachment styles is that it is not something to be "fixed" but something that can evolve with effort, understanding, emotional work, and love.

Communication Toolkit

Use these daily practice ideas below to help you practice your communication. If some seem like common sense to you, focus on the ones you know you may have trouble with.

Start small every day:
Example: Say hello to a barista, a neighbor, or a coworker and ask how their day is going. Even a 30-second conversation counts.

Use open-ended questions:
Example: Instead of asking "Did you have a good day?" ask "What was the best part of your day?" This encourages a more detailed response.

Share a little about yourself:
Example: When someone asks how your weekend was, share a funny incident or a small accomplishment, like trying a new recipe or taking a walk in the park.

Practice active listening:
Example: When a friend talks about their week, listen, and show genuine interest. "It sounds like that project was challenging. How did you handle it?" This shows you're paying attention and care about their experience.

Compliment and express gratitude:
Example: Tell a coworker, "I really appreciated how you handled that meeting today. It made things so much smoother." Or thank a friend for their advice on a small problem.

Keep it light:

Example: Share a light joke about a shared experience, like, "I think my coffee mug has a personal vendetta against me this morning." Keeping it light makes conversations feel natural and safe.

Reflect and adjust:

Example: After a conversation, think: "I could have asked more questions to show interest" or "I laughed more than usual, and I actually felt pretty good."

Daily prompts to open up:

Example: Ask a coworker or friend: "What's something you're excited about this week?" Or "What's a small win you had today?" Then share your own answer to make it reciprocal.

Track small wins:

Example: At the end of the day, write in a notebook: "I asked two people about their weekend, listened actively, and shared something funny about my day." Small victories build confidence over time.

Be patient and consistent:

Example: If a conversation feels awkward, remind yourself: "It's okay, I'm practicing. Next time will feel easier." Try again the next day, even for just a few minutes.

Chapter 10

Getting to know your Love languages

Your love language is wonderful to discover, as this can better assist you in your journey to who you are and what you like. The five love languages were created by Dr. Gary Chapman. After years of study and observations from his clients while working as a marriage counselor, he discovered that there are different ways in which one expresses and shows love. Not just in marriages and romantic partners but with families, friends, and with ourselves. When understanding these, you can then improve your communication and understanding of others and the ways they accept and give love.

Love language is how you receive and how you like to show love to other people. There are five love languages that people use within their lives. Some people may have one love language while others may have several. There are acts of service, gifts, quality time, words of affirmation, and physical touch.

1. Words of Affirmation

People with this love language feel most loved when they receive verbal praise, compliments, or encouraging words. It's about affirming someone's worth with positive, thoughtful expressions like "I love you," "You're amazing," or "I appreciate you." For them, words carry weight and can either build up or tear down.

How it affects your relationships:
If someone's love language is words of affirmation, they likely feel deeply valued when they hear kind and supportive things. Criticism or a lack of affirmation can hurt them emotionally. If this is your love language, it may also mean that you desire to receive affirmation in return to feel loved. Be mindful of how you speak to those with this language, as words can have a lasting impact.

How can you nurture this love language?
Think of someone you care about. Write them a few kind or encouraging words. A short note, a text, or even just something you want to say out loud.

Bonus: Write 3 affirmations you'd love to hear from others .
(Example: "I'm proud of you." "You make a difference." "You are loved.")

---

2. Acts of Service

Those who prefer acts of service feel loved when someone does something thoughtful to help or support them. This can include chores, running errands, or offering a helping hand. For them, actions speak louder than words, showing love through practical efforts.

How it affects your relationships:
Someone who values acts of service feels loved and cared for when someone else goes out of their way to help. On the flip side, failure to offer help can lead them to feel neglected or unimportant. If you have this love language, you may enjoy offering help in the same way. When both sides of the relationship engage in acts of service, it fosters a sense of teamwork and mutual care.

How can you nurture this love language?
Think of one simple task you can do today to help or support someone you love, or think of one simple task that can help you and support you in the future.

Bonus: What actions from others make you feel cared for?
Write 3 down.

---

3. Receiving/Giving Gifts

For people with this love language, tangible symbols of affection make them feel loved. It's not about materialism but the thought and meaning behind the gift. A small, thoughtful gesture like a favorite snack or a handwritten note can speak volumes.

How it affects your relationships:

People with this love language feel especially appreciated when they receive gifts, as it shows that others are thinking of them. If they don't receive gifts or thoughtful gestures, they may feel forgotten or unloved. If you have this love language, you might want to give love in the form of gifts, too. Understanding each other's love language can ensure thoughtful and meaningful exchanges.

How can you nurture this love language?

Give someone a small, thoughtful gift or token today; it could even be a note, a flower, or something handmade.

Bonus: Write down three gifts you've received that made you feel truly seen or appreciated.

---

4. Quality Time

Quality time involves giving your full attention to who you are with. Whether it's engaging in meaningful conversations or spending uninterrupted time together, people who value this language feel loved when they are fully present with someone. It's about connecting deeply and meaningfully.

How it affects your relationships:

If quality time is your love language, you feel most loved when you have undivided attention. Distractions, like phones or TV, can make you feel disconnected. If someone else also values this language, you may share many enriching moments together. If someone you are with doesn't focus on time together, it can leave you feeling unimportant or lonely. Whoever you are with, you will need to be mindful of each other's needs for attention and presence.

How can you nurture this love language?

Plan a small moment of intentional time with someone you care about-no distractions. It could be a walk, a shared meal, or simply sitting together and talking.

Bonus: Make a list of three ways you feel most connected during time spent with others.

---

5. Physical Touch

Physical touch is a powerful way some people experience love. Whether it's a warm hug, holding hands, a gentle back rub, or sitting close, those who value this love language feel most connected through physical presence and closeness. It's about feeling safe, seen, and supported through touch.

How it affects your relationships:

If physical touch is your love language, you likely feel most loved when someone reaches out with caring gestures. Even small forms of physical affection can make a big impact on your emotional connection. A lack of touch, or the feeling of rejection from it, can leave you feeling unwanted, distant, or emotionally isolated. If someone you care about values this language, it's important to offer touch in a way that feels respectful, consistent, and safe for both of you.

How can you nurture this love language?

Offer a meaningful, consensual gesture of physical affection to someone close to you today. This could be a hug, a hand squeeze, or simply sitting near them while talking.

Bonus: Make a list of three ways you feel most loved or connected through physical touch.

Each of these love languages is essential in how we connect with the people we care about. You understand both your own love language and someone else's. It can really help deepen your bond and make sure you both feel cared for and appreciated. It's also worth remembering that the way we express love is often the way we want to receive it, so recognizing this can really strengthen the connection in your relationships. Knowing your worth and value is also important when understanding your love language. Those who care and truly value you will try their best to understand who you are and what you value/enjoy. Those who don't or try to change you for what you value are those we may need to really place boundaries on when healing.

 ## *Self Love Questions*

1. What love languages do you resonate with? Is there more than one?

2. Do you think you show yourself love in the same way that you give love?

3. Being honest with yourself, do you believe you will be able to compromise and be open to someone who has a different love language than you?

Chapter 11

Recovery & healing
(Embrace your scars)

If you have gotten this far, you have allowed yourself or are allowing yourself to leave the past and baggage behind to move forward. It will be rocky at first, but you can do this. With any type of toxic relationship or toxic past, it is important to follow a "detachment guide" to aid you in your first steps on your journey to healing.

I personally used this guide, and even though it was tough at first, it helped me open my eyes and move forward. I encourage you again to create a self-love journal as it can deepen your healing journey. Using a self-love journal can also help you keep track of your progress and how far you have come. Remember, the only way to fully heal and move forward is through it. To fully come out the other side as the you that you deserve to be is to do the work, and although it may be painful and difficult, it will all be worth it. I promise.

Having the strength to walk away from a situation or person is not easy. You have a loving and complex heart. One day you may be ready to take the step, and then maybe one day you feel you aren't ready.

This is normal. I implore you to sit with yourself and listen to what comes up from inside your mind and your heart. Listening to only your mind can make you feel cold or rash, and listening to only your heart may make you impulsive or cause you not to see the bigger picture. Having the strength to walk away is best done when your mind and heart are in sync and are both working evenly for you to see both sides. To see and feel all your heart's wants to release while also understanding your worth and the future you want for yourself.

If this seems foreign to you, try each day to take a moment and connect with both your heart and mind. See what comes up for you in thoughts, write them down, or say them aloud. When a feeling is washing over you and comes through, feel it, welcome it, and let it out. Cry if you feel the need, laugh, sing, dance, whatever your heart is telling you to do in that moment to release and connect to who you are. By doing this, you tell your body that what you think and feel is valid and okay. Sooner or later, you will start to see the connection and communication between the mind and heart. Embracing your scars means accepting what has happened and choosing to move forward and grow from them. To sit with them and let them go. To not hold on to them and use them as a crutch for your life and your woes. Be patient with yourself and accept where you are at this moment of healing. Alchemize your pain into something beautiful.

Working with children and families on emotional regulation, I always use this activity that has helped many. I hope you can try it yourself.

I ask them to draw or write out things on their minds, things that have been weighing them down, on colorful sticky notes or paper. Afterward, we take a deep breath and we shred these. With the shreds, we create something beautiful. A picture, a rainbow, or we use them as confetti and dance. It's such a simple way to connect mind, body and heart.

Detachment guide
(To aid you in release)

1. NO contact

2. NO social media

3. Know your weaknesses and your strengths

4. Remove/discard all of their belongings

5. Self care & Self love

6. Detox your home & or space

7. Find your tribe & support system

8. Educate yourself

9. Keep your BOUNDARIES strong

Let's make a promise to yourself for yourself to help you on your journey.

I_____make a promise to myself to follow my detachment guide with what works for me. I make this promise to myself to start anew and to treat myself with respect.

I make this promise to myself to stand up for what is right and remove the people and habits in my life that are not treating and offering me the highest that I deserve.

I am loved, and I will show myself love for where I currently am on my journey. I promise from this day forward to give myself 100% of myself. To be my own best friend and give myself the love I deserve.

Sign:

Date:

1. No contact

This is #1 because it is the most important and hardest thing to do out of the whole list, NO CONTACT. This means no texting, calling, hanging out, driving by because they or you "forgot something," hanging out with their friends, family, etc. Seriously, this seems like common sense, but with a toxic relationship, it can be really difficult. The same goes for your person in mind. No answering when they call, text, or pass by your home, work, etc. Toxics may use these tactics, like showing up unexpectedly at places where you are, to show they care or, in extreme cases, to keep tabs on you. When first cutting the cords with a toxic, it's important to understand that you are not yourself. Emotionally, mentally, and maybe even physically. In extreme cases, your toxic will know this and use this to their advantage by showing up unexpectedly and/or texting and calling over and over again to restart the cycle with you.

Allow yourself the space and time to heal. Giving yourself the space and time to heal is so important. If you are able, take a day off from work, or create a weekend just for you to sit with yourself and understand what happened to you and the areas in which you believe you need to heal. In my situation, my toxic tried to keep contact with me, and they did this at my most vulnerable state.

They would send me flowers, write notes on my car, follow me home, and sit and wait outside my job and home for me. This led me down another cycle for two long years on and off with them. They would "win me back" with these gestures, and use phrases like "I won't ever do it again" and "you mean the world to me," etc. I believed it. Every single time, I believed it. The constant attention and "winning me back" would last about a month or so, and then it was back to the same old ways. Lies, manipulation, cheating, and belittling. No contact at first was difficult for me. I resorted to turning off my phone and sometimes working overtime. It helped, but not as much until I started to really dig deep and work on myself, my happiness, and my healing.

I decided to come up with the library method. If I woke up feeling vulnerable to text or contact the other person, I would "check in" my phone at a safe space or give my phone to someone I trusted to turn it off and hold it for me until I felt ready for it again, and then I would "check out" my phone. This can be a close friend, a parent, or again a safe space in your home or area that you know is a safe space for your devices. For some, this may be extreme, but for others who may need this method, I encourage you to try it.

Reminders...

1. NO contact
2. Start to think of your self-healing
3. Try the "Library method"

2. No social media

This ties in with no contact. Social media, as everyone knows, plays a major role in our lives. When moving forward from toxicity, social media needs to be cut down. Accepting your vulnerability means knowing not to fall for any traps. Don't think twice about unfollowing them and anyone else who may trigger you while you are healing. They will probably make it seem like they are doing amazing without you, or may make it seem that they are miserable without you. Both will be doors that will lead you down the same roller coaster. Gloating on how amazing they are doing or not doing is to get your reaction to A) get upset and say something, or B) make you feel like they maybe do care for you and have you crawl back. BOTH lead you back to them. This is the goal. To avoid both, make this choice easy and just unfollow.

Over time, after keeping these rules in play, they may slowly stop and fade from view, or there will be the chance that you will get the occasional DM or like on your story or post. Once again, all are free invites on that roller coaster. It is your choice if you decide to go on. This journey may not be easy. It wasn't for me. You must keep pushing. You are strong.

Reminders...

1. Ignore, cut off, & break these ties
2. Don't sit on the roller coaster

3. Remove/discard all of their belongings

This will correlate with (number 6) later in this chapter. Removing and discarding their belongings is a tricky thing to do. What may first come to mind is to give back all belongings to your toxic. This is where it gets tricky. Whether you are in contact or no contact with them, I will leave it up to you to either throw out the items or store everything in a big garbage bag, label it, and place it somewhere unseen, or leave it somewhere for them to retrieve. This is in case they find a way and decide to ask for their items. Stay strong and understand that if they use phrases like "I want to see you one last time" or "Why can't you give them to me?" then they may be using a manipulation tactic to see you again. To start the cycle. If they don't contact you in about four to six months for their items, then remove the items. If there are shared-property, legal, or valuable items involved, take steps that protect you while following the law, and use a third party if needed.

The important thing is to remove these items from your space to begin your healing and new days ahead. Don't contact them about their belongings; this will most likely start the cycle up over again. If gathering their personal items is difficult, this is where your support system (Number 7) comes in handy for your healing.

Reminders...

1. Their items can be reminders of your pain
2. Use a support system to help with removal

4. Knowing your weaknesses and your strengths

Taking the time to sit with yourself to note all your strengths and weaknesses will allow you to see exactly the areas where you need to work. Maybe it is a piece of cake to keep and hold the no-contact rule, but when it comes to throwing away their favorite sweater they left at your house, you just cannot seem to go through with it.

Taking a step back to reflect on why you have these strengths and weaknesses may also help. Maybe by taking that step back and really thinking about it, you begin to see where your self-worth was smaller than it should have been, where you accepted less than you deserved, or where you held on because part of you was still learning how to choose yourself. You may also be able to see where you are comfortable and where you still need some help in releasing.

Reminders...

1. Note your strengths and weaknesses
2. See where and how you can get help for your weaknesses
3. Are there any "aha" moments where you feel you could be taken advantage of?

Expressive exercise

Take a piece of paper and fold it hot dog style. On one side, write down all your strengths.

On the other side, write out all your weaknesses.

Next to your weaknesses, try to write out why you have those, and when you think they came to be. Childhood? An experience? A traumatic event?

Maybe it's this current relationship we are focusing on for you. Pinpointing each weakness and getting to the root cause is the start of your new, healthy, beautiful journey.

Nipping these weaknesses will create space for new strengths and lessons to form.

From here, decide whether you can work on these on your own or if you need support (family, friends, a psychologist, a therapist, etc.)

5. Self care & Self love

The biggest steps to healing begin with self-love and self-care.
If you don't take care of yourself, how can you possibly think of
moving forward and beginning anew? Creating space for yourself
to love yourself is imperative for healing. Make a list of all your
current hobbies and any new hobbies or things that you have
always wanted to do or start doing again. Allow yourself time in
the week/month to start these hobbies. Make this healing journey
about you and you alone. It is not selfish to want to heal and
become the person you have always
wanted to be.

Reminders...

1. Who do you want to be a year from now?
2. How can you show yourself love?
3. How can you show yourself self care?
4. You are worth the time and effort to grow and heal

If you could have a day all to yourself, what would it look
like? From when you wake up until when you go to sleep?

6. Detox your home & or space

Create a new, clean space in your home to allow for a new outlook on the future. I did this by clearing out all old items, which reminded me of my past, and were items I no longer needed or wanted to create space for something new. This could be anything from books, clothes, furniture, loose papers, even blankets and bed sheets. The goal of this is to have a space in your home that is clean, fresh, and new for the fresh and new you. Coming home after a rough day to a space where you can unwind and focus on the positive is the aim. What sounds better? A home/space with everything that reminds you of your pain and past? OR, a home/space with everything new and fresh, reminding you of your strength and bravery for the future ahead?

List 3 things you can think of to get rid of in your home/space right now.

1.

2.

3.

7. Find your tribe & support system

Having those who love and support you during this healing journey can allow you to heal faster, and with more love & support comes more room and openness to heal. Your family, friends, and a support group with others like yourself are all amazing options for a support system. Make sure your support system is non-judgmental. Is open to your story and your wounds and will be there 100% to help guide and lift you. Picking the right support system can be challenging. Here is what to look for... Someone who is open to your story. Someone who will not judge you and your past. Someone who can be there for you without the projection of their own opinions or story onto you. Someone who loves and or cares for you equally and mutually and is open to being a support system and ladder for you and your growth.

List 3 support systems

1.

2.

3.

8. Educate yourself

This was by far one of the best things I did for my healing. Educating myself about what happened to me, who I was, and why I accepted what I did. I can't say this enough... BOOKS, BOOKS, BOOKS. Books, courses, and research led me to understand all the questions I had and led me to write this book myself for you. To help aid and guide others. I will list all my book recommendations in the back of this book, but many amazing books like...

The Psychopath Inside -by James Fallon
The Body Keeps the Score -by Bessel van der Kolk, M.D.
It Didn't Start with You -by Mark Wolynn

These books opened my eyes to the details of my past and guided me in healing for today. These books all provide eye-opening facts and can help you understand the deepest details of your toxic and past traumas down to brain activity and adolescence, as well as who you are as a whole. Body, mind, and soul.

List 3 books of interest here

1.

2.

3.

9. Keep your BOUNDARIES strong!

Boundaries are one of the most powerful tools you can use to protect your well-being. They are the lines you draw to preserve your emotional, mental, and physical space from being invaded by others. Setting boundaries for yourself is about honoring your own needs, desires, and limits, without feeling guilty or overwhelmed by the needs of those around you. When you set strong boundaries, you're essentially telling yourself that your well-being is important. It's about creating a space where you can thrive, feel at peace, and be your authentic self, without constantly bending over backward to meet others' demands.

For many of us, learning to set boundaries is a gradual process. It means recognizing when something or someone is draining your energy or making you feel uncomfortable. Whether it's saying "no" to that extra shift at work, something that doesn't serve you, stepping away from toxic relationships, or taking time to rest when you need it, boundaries are all about choosing yourself. This might mean telling a friend you need some time for yourself, setting limits on your work hours, or not engaging in conversations that feel emotionally draining.

Setting boundaries is also about acknowledging that your needs matter. It's easy to fall into the trap of people-pleasing or putting others before yourself, but when you neglect your own boundaries, it can lead to burnout, resentment, and feelings of being overwhelmed.

It's important to recognize that taking care of yourself is not selfish; it's essential for your mental health and overall well-being. And, while it may feel uncomfortable at first, the more you practice setting and enforcing boundaries, the easier it becomes.

Boundaries aren't about shutting people out or creating distance; they're about creating a healthy space where you can nurture yourself and your relationships. When you have clear boundaries, you can engage with others from a place of strength and clarity, rather than from a place of exhaustion or resentment. By respecting your own boundaries, you're teaching others to do the same, ensuring that your relationships are based on mutual respect and understanding.

Ultimately, boundaries are a form of self-love. They show that you're worthy of love and respect, and that you don't need to sacrifice your peace or happiness for anyone else.

Setting boundaries is an ongoing practice, but each time you assert them, you're reinforcing your commitment to honoring yourself and creating the life you truly deserve.

An experience I'd like to share is when I finally broke it off with my toxic ex. Years of manipulation and cheating finally made me snap back into reality. He knew it was over because I had never placed a no-contact boundary before. Because I did this, he started showing up at my home and dropping off flowers.

Each day, the flower bouquet would get bigger and bigger, and then it began to come with letters. When I still didn't respond, he would then start to show up around my neighborhood and my house unexpectedly. It became quite scary, actually. Not knowing if I would be safe walking out of my own home was unsettling. One evening I was out with my mother, and when we were arriving home, he was lingering outside the house. We had to drive around and wait for him to leave. This went on for months.

I was annoyed, obviously upset, and actually disgusted. That finally, when I decided to stand up for myself, he showed up. Looking back now, I know 1000% that I did the right thing. It was the turning point of my healing that I needed to become who I am today by sticking to my boundaries and showing myself respect.

After this, he began using social media to have others speak with me. People would send me screenshots of his Instagram stories and sob story posts. Posting things with my full name to get attention. He went as far as getting a tattoo as a remembrance of me. As if I had died. I did die, though; I killed off the parts of myself that didn't serve me and the parts that I outgrew. I elevated, educated myself, healed, and I am a completely different person. All for the better. All because I chose myself.

Keep moving forward,

&

you'll never have a reason to look
back.

Self Love Questions

1. What boundaries can you put in place right now with yourself during your time of healing?

2. How about with others?

3. Out of all these points in the detachment guide, which one do you think you will definitely be using?

You are like a work of art. Not everyone will understand you, but those who do, will never forget you.

Chapter 12

Moving forward

As time rolls along, your pain and hurt will move on as long as you take the step to push forward. Dwelling on the past and what could have been or what you could have done differently will drive you mad. When moving forward from your past, working on yourself is a big chunk of how you will grow to become your future self. Learning when people (don't fit) and learning from your past experiences will help you get there. When moving forward, remember to surround yourself with people who genuinely love you and care for you.

Moving forward from a traumatic past will take time, but you will grow and see the changes. When meeting new people, being open and telling them about your healing journey and where you are on it is a great exercise to build trust. When healing, you may say things or do things that are out of your character. Being open with others allows us to build better connections with people who will be supportive of us and our healing. You will be surprised when meeting someone new that they have probably had similar experiences and journeys to yours.

When moving forward, remember to be gentle and patient with yourself. When you finally leave a toxic relationship, people often say, "I'm so proud of you," or "You're so strong." And you are. Truly. You made it out of something that was slowly chipping away at your spirit, and that takes courage.

But what most people don't see is what happens next. They don't talk about the quiet. The strange stillness after the storm. The moment when the adrenaline wears off, and the silence feels too loud. They don't talk about the confusion, the questions, the ache you can't quite name.

Leaving was the first step. A huge one. But healing? Healing is the journey that follows.

And it's not always what we expect.

Emotional Whiplash

At first, you might feel a mix of everything and nothing. One moment you're overwhelmed with sadness, anger, or even guilt. Then next, you feel completely numb. You may float through your days, going through the motions, wondering why freedom feels so unfamiliar. This is normal. Your heart is catching its breath.

Anxiety and Over-Alertness

After being in survival mode for so long, it can be hard to convince your body that it's safe now. You might find yourself jumping at small noises, overthinking conversations, or constantly preparing for something bad to happen. That's just your nervous system trying to protect you. It's doing what it was trained to do. Over time, with patience and safety, it will learn a new rhythm.

Guilt, shame, and all the "Should've"

You might find yourself thinking, "I should've left sooner," or "Why did I let it get so far?" But here's the thing: you did the best you could with what you knew, in the situation you were in. No one plans to lose themselves inside someone else's storm. The guilt you feel is not a sign of weakness; it's a sign that you cared. That you believed in love. That's nothing to be ashamed of.

Grieving the love you hoped for

Even in toxic relationships, there are moments that feel real. Promises made, dreams shared. You might find yourself missing those moments, even if you know they weren't healthy. That's okay. Grief is complicated. You're not just grieving the relationship; you're grieving the version of love you hoped it could be or the person you wished they would be for you. And that's a loss worth honoring.

Losing yourself, then slowly finding you again

After being controlled, criticized, or constantly walking on eggshells, you might not recognize yourself. Your confidence may feel shattered. You might have forgotten what you love, what you enjoy, and what makes you feel alive. That's okay. You're not lost; you're just buried under years of survival. Bit by bit, you'll find your way back to the soft, strong person you've always been.

The Little (and Big) Things That Might Show Up

Let's talk about the traits and patterns that can linger after leaving
a toxic relationship, not because you're broken, but because
healing takes time. These are not flaws.
They are the marks of a nervous system learning to feel safe again.

You may notice:

Constant self-doubt – You second-guess yourself, even with
small decisions. Your intuition is still waking back up.

Low self-esteem – It's hard to feel confident when someone has
made you question your worth for so long.

People-pleasing – You might find yourself saying "yes" when you
want to say "no," trying to keep the peace, avoid conflict, or feel
accepted.

Over-apologizing – "Sorry" might come out of your mouth
without thinking. You've trained yourself to believe you are
always in the wrong.

Fear of conflict – Even small disagreements might send your
heart racing. You're still learning that not all conflict is dangerous.

Trouble setting boundaries – Boundaries may feel foreign or
even selfish at first. But you'll get there.

Difficulty trusting – Not just others, but yourself too. But trust is
like a muscle. It gets stronger with use.

Emotional flashbacks – Little things may unexpectedly bring up big feelings. A tone of voice. A memory. A smell. It can be disorienting, but you're safe now, and those moments will pass.

The Stillness After the Storm- After chaos, it can be strange to find peace. When you've spent so much time walking on eggshells, trying to stay safe, or waiting for the next emotional storm, calm can feel... uncomfortable. You may even call it boredom.

But what you're feeling isn't boredom. It's your nervous system learning how to rest. For so long, it's been in survival mode, used to adrenaline, tension, and uncertainty. When that constant state of alertness fades, the quiet can feel foreign. You might start to wonder if something is missing, or if the lack of intensity means what your feeling (love, happiness) isn't real.

In truth, that "missing spark" is often the absence of chaos. It's your body and mind adjusting to safety. Healthy love doesn't trigger the highs and lows you once mistook for passion; it brings steadiness, trust, and peace.

Those who grew up in unpredictable or toxic environments may find that stillness almost feels suspicious at first, as if peace can't be trusted.

This phase of healing is asking you to slow down and relearn what love feels like when it's not built on fear/stress. To recognize that peace is not the same as boredom. It's the feeling of being safe enough to exhale. In time, your body will begin to recognize that this ease is what love was always meant to feel like.

And yes...

You may also experience physical symptoms:

1. Exhaustion, even after sleeping

2. Headaches or body tension

3. Changes in appetite

4. Trouble sleeping

5. A general sense of feeling "off"

6. Numbness (feeling nothing)

7. Feeling too many emotions at once

8. Physical sickness (like a cold or flu)

This is your body processing months or years of stress and fear. Be gentle with it. Rest is healing.

But here's the magic part...

As time goes on, slowly, and maybe suddenly, you begin to change.

Self-Awareness blossoms- You start noticing what you need, what you don't want, what no longer fits. You catch yourself before falling into old patterns. You begin to trust your voice again, even when it shakes.

You become softer and stronger- There's a new tenderness in how you see the world. A quiet strength in how you carry yourself. You're less afraid to take up space, to speak your truth, to say, "This isn't okay."

You crave realness- After all the lies, games, and gaslighting, you want truth. You want kindness that doesn't come with strings. You want peace that doesn't feel like walking on eggshells.

You begin to rebuild- Slowly, you rediscover joy. You laugh without checking who's watching. You dance in your kitchen. You reconnect with hobbies, passions, and dreams that were pushed aside. You begin to bloom in places you once thought were barren.

You are not broken. You are becoming- Healing doesn't happen all at once. It comes in waves. Some days you'll feel powerful, like you can conquer anything. Other days, you'll curl up and cry. oth are part of the process. Both are sacred.

Healing isn't linear, which means that your healing journey may not be all sunshine and rainbows. There will be days and maybe weeks when you take a step back from healing or when you stumble, fall, and have to start this journey where you left off or even from the start again.

If you think you've fully healed, one day something may trigger an emotion, response, or memory that you weren't prepared for. Trusting in yourself and understanding that you are the greatest project you will work on and that you are still in this healing process will allow you to give yourself grace and compassion for where you are. Even today, I am still healing from childhood experiences and fears that come up from my past that trickle into my present. To truly heal is to accept what has happened and choose differently for yourself in the now.

So if you're sitting in the middle of the mess, wondering when it gets better, this is your reminder: it already is better. Because you're no longer living in that pain. You're moving through it. You're choosing yourself again and again.

You're not just surviving... You're growing.

You're learning how to love yourself in all the ways you once begged someone else to.

You're not too much. You're not too sensitive. You're not weak.

You are healing.

So take a deep breath and know you've got this. It takes a strong person to choose this journey of healing and change.

If you have made it this far, you are a very beautiful, wise, and strong soul indeed.

PART IV

Self-Love & Integration

——— ✳ ———

You are home in youself.

Chapter 13

The mini self love guide

Within the process of healing is a lot of work, patience, and dedication to yourself for yourself. I encourage you to create a monthly chart. Pick some of these from each category and try them. Maybe pick one a week, or one a day, as much healing as you think you need and want to begin with.

How to create a self-love guide

- Use the categories listed and focus on the ones you feel you need the most work on.
- Create a monthly log of your ideas and what you would like to try.
- After trying each activity, use a journal to write your progress. How you felt before and after an activity from this guide.
- Use the ideas from this guide that you enjoy the most and begin to implement them into your regular day-to -day life.
- * Know that using these tools and allowing yourself to heal and grow will make space for healthier and more fulfilling relationships and opportunities.

Healing from a toxic relationship, whether it be a partner, parent, friend, work situation, or other, we need to take into account all forms of our being. Physical, mental, emotional, and spiritual.

I created self-love ideas for you to utilize on your journey. I hope these help you as they have helped me.

Physical

1. Begin a yoga practice (five to ten minutes to start).

2. Try some deep breathing practices (5-finger breaths).

3. When you first wake up, stretch and hug yourself.

4. After waking, go outside for at least 10-15 minutes. Allow for some grounding. Walk barefoot in the grass or dirt. Listen to nature and the sounds around you. Just be for a while.

5. Try a new hobby: biking, painting, gardening, sewing, reading, cooking, building, etc.

6. Sleep in: Turn off your alarms and your notifications. Sleep in the late morning and wake up when your body is ready.

7. Get to know yourself - look in the mirror for five or ten minutes and find the details of who you are. Only show positive love by giving yourself a couple of compliments on how you look and what makes you unique.

8. Even if you are going to run small errands or stay in the house, dress up for yourself. This will boost your confidence and make you more in touch with your likes, dislikes, and who you are.

9. Work out, join a fitness class, and get your body moving through dance, sports, etc. (It's never too late to start something. There are adult classes for everything! Even ballet.)

10. Create a vision board - How do you see your life in the next year or two? What are your hopes, dreams, and wants? Make a board depicting all your goals and hang it up somewhere you can reflect on it every day.

11. Buy yourself flowers and display them in your house, office, or workspace proudly.

12. Eat something delicious: chocolate, pizza, wings, ice cream. Indulge and treat yourself to your favorite foods.

13. Clean out your space. Remove all items from a part of your home that you believe no longer serves you. You can start small. For example, try a closet that's been accumulating junk or the kitchen with all those mugs you know you'll never use. A clean space allows for fresh, new memories and a space for relaxed, healthy thoughts.

14. Practice for even five minutes a day to sit in stillness and tune in to your body. Listen and try to distinguish what your body is telling you. Are you hungry, thirsty, stressed, or tired? The more you do this, the easier it will be to understand your body and connect fully with it.

15. Try a massage or other special treatment. If you are open, make an appointment to get a massage or get a pedicure/manicure. *When I first started on my journey, it was very, very hard to have anyone touch me physically. I dove in and treated myself to my first manicure, and it changed my self-confidence and trust in others.

16. Practice good posture. Sit up tall when working, remember to drop your shoulders, and unclench your jaw. Walking with proper posture and a head held high really does boost your confidence. Look at yourself in the mirror while trying this and notice how your body feels.

17. Create and establish healthy boundaries. Begin by walking away physically from uncomfortable situations or people. Don't overwork yourself; take breaks when needed to avoid burnout.

18. Buy a new outfit: within your budget, of course.

19. Attempt to have a solo mini trip somewhere local (staycation).

20. Show up for a group event, make new friends, and be yourself.

Mental/Emotional

1. Read a book focused on your healing at least thirty minutes.

2. Listen to a podcast on healing and self love (e.g., *The lavendaire lifestyle* on Spotify/Youtube).

3. Begin daily gratitude. List five things you are grateful for each day.

4. Practice mindful mornings. Stay away from your phone for at least thirty minutes when waking, make your bed, and let some sunshine in.

5. Surround yourself with friends and family that lift your spirits. Spend some quality time with them.

6. Ask for help. Asking for help is a sign of strength not weakness.

7. Listen to your heart and mind. Find the balance between the two, and if you need a self-care day, time off, or a day alone, take one!

8. Set boundaries with people, places, old hobbies, or habits that no longer serve the new you.

9. Trust your gut. Literally. Remember that your nervous system and body are connected. Your first intuitions matter. Practice listening to your first thoughts and feelings when you're around new people and places.

10. Say "no" when you don't want to do something. Mean what you say and stand firm with your words.

11. Sit in quiet for 5 minutes. Let your thoughts come and go. This is important to healing, as many people use technology to "drown out the noise of thoughts." Add 5 minutes to this once you get the hang of things.

12. Try an anger-releasing activity with family, friends, or yourself. Go to a rage room (a safe place where you smash and break objects) and let it all go.

13. Give yourself permission to heal from the same thing twice or more. Healing isn't the same for all.

14. Use a journal prompt from the list in this book. Dedicate yourself to writing in each journal prompt every day or once a week for reflection.

15. Read affirmations in the morning or right before bed to set the mood for the hours ahead.

16. Create a mood music playlist with positive songs and artists.

17. If you feel like crying... cry.

18. Mental loads can sometimes weigh more than physical ones, so again, ask for help. The strongest people do.

19. Begin to hold space for daily reviews of your feelings, manifestations, goals, and events for the end of each day. Keep track of how much you've grown.

20. Understand that progress and growth may take some time. Be accepting of where you are and what you need to work on. Make mistakes and be okay with knowing that it's okay.

Spiritual

*This can look different for everyone.
These are some examples.*

1. Attend a service that's a part of your faith.

2. Dabble in tarot and get to know yourself.

3. Visit your local church and sit awhile.

4. Volunteer at a local food/toy drive.

5. Listen to your favorite sermon.

6. Attend a fun spiritual workshop.

7. If you don't have a faith but want to explore, read holy texts from different ones (ex- Quran, Bible, Gita, Torah, Tripitaka)

8. Attend a full moon circle.

9. Take time to create a prayer routine.

10. Look up the meaning of the signs the universe might be sending your way.

11. Listen to uplifting music (faith-inspired)

12. Light a candle with intention and sit with your thoughts, prayers, or hopes.

Self Love Questions

What 10 things from the Self Love Guide will you
dedicate yourself to try? List them below

1.

2.

3.

4.

5.

6.

7.

8.

9.

10.

No.

Is a complete sentence

Chapter 14

Where happiness lies

Happiness and the things that fulfill us are different for everyone. Some might say money, some might say seeing the world, and some might say people. The treasure at the end of all healing is realizing and truly understanding that happiness is only found within yourself. You can be a millionaire, travel to every continent on the planet, have a thousand friends, but at the end of the night, when you put your head on your pillow, if you are not happy with yourself, nothing and no one in the world will be able to fill that space. Until you see that only you can really fill your own happiness meter before all else, you will not be able to heal properly, and you will never be truly happy.

To understand true happiness within yourself, we must look deep into who you are on a basic level, the essence of your mind, personality, spirit, energy, whatever fits you best. You are unique and unlike anyone else. Like a fingerprint specially marked, you are marked with your own unique likes, dislikes, skills, thoughts, and opinions. Accepting all of you for who you are is the start of true happiness.

Is there something you used to do, or a way you used to act that you have stopped because someone else or society's opinion told you it wasn't the "right way," "best way," or way that the other person wanted you to be? Open up those parts of yourself and tell yourself that it's okay to be you.

I remember trying my best to tiptoe around any situation to not make a stir and forming myself to act like someone who was not me. Saying certain phrases and sharing beliefs that I did not agree with to make someone else and the society I was a part of happy and content. I wanted to fit in, and I wanted my toxics happiness. But was I happy? Leaving that situation made me realize how much I missed myself. The parts of me that I was born with that I pushed away because of someone else's opinion, and to make someone else happy. I remember looking in the mirror and not recognizing myself. I had to stand there and reintroduce myself to myself. Baby steps, then jumps, then leaps. It started with noticing the freckles on my face, remembering my favorite color and what I loved to eat, and rediscovering that I once loved to figure skate, write
poems, make jewelry, and create.

The list will grow, and it does take time. It took me a month to remember my favorite color and almost 6 months to feel okay sharing my thoughts, hanging out with friends again. Everyone's journey is different, but the end is all the same. You reach the finish line, and you become YOU again. You fall in love with yourself and see the world in such a beautiful light. What happened to you will be a stepping stone or a big-ass staircase that you climbed and moved on from. The only thing standing between you and your healing now is your relationship with yourself. So where do you begin? You begin by reconnecting with who you truly are. Start by listening. Start by remembering. Start by allowing yourself to meet yourself again.

What's your favorite color? How many freckles are on your face? Do you even have any? What's your favorite food? What is your favorite show? Part of my healing was buying a book called *The ME journal.*

It is a pocket-sized book filled with either-or questions and fill-in-the-blank questions just like this. The book was created to write about your life so you can have it as a keepsake for your future family. I used it for my healing, and some questions are as small as "Do you prefer morning or night?" and "Do you like salty or sweet food?" I was stuck on it for quite a while. I encourage everyone to find this book to help you begin your discovery of who you are.

A big part of a toxic relationship is manipulation. Many of us have been conditioned to believe that we need a certain person in order to live a functioning life, even when that person is hurting us. But you do not need someone who keeps your nervous system in constant overdrive. Anyone in your life who makes your palms sweat, your legs shake, your stomach or head hurt, your voice tremble, or your heart race may not belong in your inner circle. We are often taught, especially as children and teens, that if our body reacts strongly to someone, it must mean there is a deep connection, that they are "the one." Sometimes it is just excitement or nerves, wanting to make a good impression. But sometimes it is your nervous system trying to tell you that something is wrong.

Your happiness should live where your body can soften, not tighten. You should feel calm, safe, relaxed, and fully yourself around the people in your life.

Some forms of manipulation show up as dependency, patterns that may have been taught to you by another person. This can look like needing them for day to day activities, for going to the store, for using the car, or for having them in charge of all the household or shared finances. This is not healthy, and it is important to see it clearly. Part of creating happiness for yourself is remembering that you are capable.

You do not need to be in a relationship to be whole. It is okay to be alone for a while. It is okay to rebuild your life without centering it around another person. Learning to stand on your own again is not loneliness. It is strength.

You are capable of taking these steps and so much more. Start small if you need to. Go to the store alone, then a restaurant, then the movies, and maybe even take a trip by yourself. These are all ways to rebuild your independence and your self trust, for who you are now and who you are becoming.

"No one can make you feel inferior without your consent."
— Eleanor Roosevelt

A Moment to Reflect

Take another deep breath.

This is your space and a pause to reconnect with yourself.

So often in toxic relationships, we lose sight of our own needs, our voice, our small joys. Healing begins when we start asking ourselves gentle questions. Not to judge, but to remember who we are underneath all the noise.

Reflection is an act of love. It helps us see where we've been, what we've learned, and where we still want to grow. Take your time with these questions. You don't need perfect answers, only honesty and kindness toward yourself.

Sit quietly with your thoughts. Let your heart speak.

Take these questions with you.

Whisper them to yourself during quiet moments, answer them here, or carry the ones that call to you throughout the day.

The more you listen inward, the more you'll realize you've had the answers all along.

You are becoming your own safe place.

Reflection Questions

1. When was the last time you did something just for yourself? Not to please or impress anyone, but simply because it made you feel good?

2. When was the last time you took a quiet walk, without your phone, just to breathe and notice the world around you?

3. What makes you feel most at peace? When was the last time you allowed yourself to be in that place or moment?

4. What parts of yourself have you been hiding to feel loved or accepted by others?

5. What does respect mean to you, and how can you start giving more of it to yourself every day?

6. When was the last time you said "no" without explaining yourself, and how did it feel?

7. What small habit or routine helps you reconnect with yourself when you start to feel lost or drained?

8. What do you need to forgive yourself for so you can move forward with softness instead of guilt?

9. Who in your life makes you feel safe, seen, and at ease? How can you spend more time on that energy?

10. What does happiness mean to you now, and how has your definition of it changed as you've learned to love yourself?

11. What would your life look like if you fully trusted yourself. our intuition, your timing, your worth? What would you stop doing? What would you start?

12. In what areas of your life are you settling for "comfortable" instead of choosing what truly feels aligned and expansive?

13. If you treated yourself with the same compassion and patience you offer others, what would change in your daily life?

14. What emotions have you been avoiding lately, and what might they be trying to teach you if you allowed yourself to feel them fully?

15. If your body could speak to you right now, what would it ask for more of? What would it ask you to release?

Chapter 15
Journal prompts for healing

There are 30 prompts for 30 days of healing. Try one each day to aid you in your healing journey.

Journaling can be a major help when it comes to healing. Releasing your thoughts and feelings on paper can assist you to help you in feeling lighter. This is a perfect opportunity to put to the test the tools mentioned. Find some free time each day, find or buy a beautiful journal, light some candles, make some tea or coffee and create time for yourself each day.

1. Describe a challenging experience and explore what it taught you and how it has shaped you.

2. List three things you are grateful for today.

3. Write a letter to your younger self. Offering support and advice. *Make sure not to turn this into a "I wish I didn't" moment.

4. Explore positive affirmations. Write down which three resonate with you and describe why.

5. Write about a person who has positively impacted your life.

6. Describe a place that gives you tranquility and peace.

7. Write about a hobby or activity that brings you happiness. If you don't have one, write about one that you would like to try and why.

8. Write about a moment when you showed yourself kindness and how it felt.

9. Write down three things you need to let go of to create more space for self-love in your life.

10. Focusing on self-forgiveness, write a letter to yourself, releasing any guilt and shame that may have built up inside.

11. When you have your self-care day, document it, and write about how your day went, how you felt, and what was the best parts.

12. Write down the qualities of your close family or friends that you appreciate the most.

13. Write about a moment that you felt truly aligned in your life and how you felt.

14. Journal about a time you stepped out of your comfort zone.

15. Write a gratitude letter to your past self about how proud and grateful you are for all of your accomplishments.

16. Reflect on a favorite childhood memory and what made it so special.

17. Focus on three goals you have for yourself this year. Write them in detail, including how you would feel when you complete them.

18. Write about your favorite self-help book, podcast, or show that has helped you change or influence your mindset.

19. Focusing on forgiveness, write a letter to someone you need to forgive. Keep this as a reminder that forgiveness and healing are possible.

20. Write a letter to yourself at the beginning of your healing journey and compare where you are now to when you feel like you've progressed.

21. List some activities you love to do to help you feel a sense of calm. Why do you like these activities?

22. Plan a self-love solo trip. This can be as small as going to the movies or a bakery alone, to a spa day, or traveling somewhere new. Plan out every detail. Indulge and include all the ways you will show yourself love.

23. Journal about a time you said "no" and meant it. Describe what it was about and how it felt to stick to your word and respect yourself.

24. Write about how your childhood was. Describe all the ways your childhood may have created positive and/or
negative behaviors in who you are now.
or a job change.

25. Describe your dream life in extreme detail. What you are doing, where you are, and who you are with. Use this as a manifestation tool to push you to make this life a reality. Reread this when you feel any doubt.

26. Plan and schedule. How would you like to live your life each day? Is it walking every morning? Yoga after work? Write down your perfect daily schedule and try to implement this in your life.

27. Take time to reflect and release all the things that are taking up your thoughts today.

28. Draw a roadmap with squares or blocks. Write down any milestones you accomplish on this road to healing. At the end of your roadmap, draw a castle or whatever the goal/end point looks like to you. Decorate this page and revisit it often for reflection.

29. Make a list of all the things in your life that give you joy,from the smallest things like your coffee to something big like a move or a job change.

30. Make a list of all the things you refuse to accept in life and from any relationship from this day forward.

YOUR HEALING
ISN'T LINEAR
SO CHOOSE

YOU

EVERY STEP
OF THE WAY

Final words

If you take one thing from this book, let it be this: You were never hard to love, just giving your love to people who couldn't hold it.

Self-love isn't about perfection or constant confidence. It's about coming home to yourself after every storm. It's about choosing peace over chaos, boundaries over approval, and truth over illusions. Healing is not linear, and neither is growth. Some days you'll feel strong, and others you'll feel the ache of what once was. But every time you choose yourself, you reclaim a piece of your power.

You are not what they did to you. You are the person who survived, who learned, and who is now rewriting the story with love, softness, and strength.

Here's to the version of you that decided: "I deserve better." Because you do. And you always have.

Thank You

To the hearts who stayed when it hurt, who kept giving until they had nothing left, and still found the courage to start again. To my friends and family who believed in my voice when I doubted it, thank you for holding space for me to grow, write, and heal.

And most importantly, to YOU, the reader: thank you for being here. For choosing to turn inward. For daring to believe that love begins with you.

May this book be a reminder that you are whole, worthy, and free to build a life that feels like peace.

Chapter 16
Index for healing

This guide includes hotlines, books, podcasts, and websites that I personally recommend to support you on your healing journey. Many of these resources have helped me along the way, and I hope they can offer you comfort, clarity, and support as well. My hope is that this book has helped you in some small or meaningful way as you move toward a brighter, healthier future for your sacred self.

If you'd like to learn more about my work with Self Sacred®, visit:
Yourselfsacred.com
Instagram: @self_ sacred

Follow along for retreats, updates, and more from Self Sacred®

Books

The Body Keeps the Score- by Bessel van der Kolk, MD

Healing from Trauma and Abuse- by Janine L. F. Laird

It Didn't Start with You- by Mark Wolynn

The Power of Now- by Eckhart Tolle

You Can Heal Your Life- by Louise Hay

Complex PTSD: From Surviving to Thriving- by Pete Walker

The Self-Love Experiment- by Shannon Kaiser

The Four Agreements- by Don Miguel Ruiz

The Me Journal- a questionnaire keepsake

Healing Isn't Linear (this book)

Podcasts / Music

Lavendaire Lifestyle- by Aileen Xu

The Trauma Therapist Podcast- by Guy Macpherson

The Mindful Kind- by Rachael Kable

The Mindset Mentor- by Rob Dial

The Feel Good Effect- by Robyn Conley

Unlearn- by Kelly McNelis

Self Love Affirmations- Spotify/YouTube

Zen Meditations- Spotify/YouTube

Hotlines

1. National Suicide Prevention Lifeline (U.S.)
Phone Number: 988 (Available 24/7)
Website: https://988lifeline.org/
Focus: Immediate help for individuals experiencing suicidal thoughts, emotional distress, or mental health crises.

2. Crisis Text Line
Phone Number: Text HOME to 741741 (Available 24/7)
Website: https://www.crisistextline.org/
Focus: Text-based support for people in crisis, offering mental health resources and emotional support through text.

3. National Domestic Violence Hotline (U.S.)
Phone Number: 1-800-799-SAFE (1-800-799-7233)
Website: https://www.thehotline.org/
Focus: Assistance and resources for those experiencing domestic violence, including immediate help and long-term support.

4. National Helpline for Sexual Assault (RAINN)
Phone Number: 1-800-656-HOPE (1-800-656-4673)
Website: https://www.rainn.org/
Focus: Support for survivors of sexual assault, providing confidential services, including a 24/7 hotline.

5. Veterans Crisis Line (U.S.)
Phone Number: 1-800-273-8255 (Press 1 for veterans)
Text: Text 838255
Website: https://www.veteranscrisisline.net/
Focus: Dedicated crisis support for veterans, service members, and their families.

6. National Eating Disorders Association (NEDA) Helpline
Website: https://www.nationaleatingdisorders.org/
Focus: Provides support, resources, and information for those struggling with eating disorders and related issues.

7. LGBTQ+ National Hotline (The Trevor Project)
Phone Number: 1-866-488-7386
Text: Text START to 678678
Website: https://www.thetrevorproject.org/
Focus: Confidential support for LGBTQ+ individuals facing crisis, mental health challenges, or emotional distress.

8. SAMHSA National Helpline (Substance Abuse and Mental Health)
Phone Number: 1-800-662-HELP (1-800-662-4357)
Website: https://www.samhsa.gov/find-help/national-helpline
Focus: Provides free, confidential help and resources for individuals dealing with substance use and mental health disorders.

9. National Runaway Safeline
Phone Number: 1-800-RUNAWAY (1-800-786-2929)
Website: https://www.1800runaway.org/
Focus: A 24/7 confidential resource for runaway youth, offering crisis support and guidance for individuals in need of emergency assistance.

10. Mental Health America
Phone Number: 1-800-969-6642 (Helpline)
Website: https://www.mhanational.org/
Focus: Offers support and resources for mental health education, advocacy, and crisis intervention.

Sites

1. Psychology Today
Website: https://www.psychologytoday.com/
Focus: Directory of licensed therapists, psychologists, and counselors. It also offers articles and resources on mental health topics, including self-love and trauma recovery.

2. BetterHelp
Website: https://www.betterhelp.com/
Focus: Online therapy and counseling services. BetterHelp connects individuals with licensed therapists via text, video, and phone calls.

3. Talkspace
Website: https://www.talkspace.com/
Focus: Online therapy platform where users can receive mental health support and therapy through text, video, and audio messaging.

4. Self-Care Besties
Website: https://www.selfcarebesties.com/
Focus: Provides support for building self-love practices, healing from trauma, and establishing a solid foundation of self-care.

5. The Recovery Village
Website: https://www.therecoveryvillage.com/
Focus: Offers resources on addiction, mental health treatment, and rehabilitation, including trauma recovery and self-care programs.

6. National Alliance on Mental Illness (NAMI)
Website: https://www.nami.org/
Focus: Offers resources for individuals affected by mental illness, including educational materials and ways to connect with support groups for emotional and mental health.

7. Trauma-Informed Care
Website: https://www.traumainformedcareproject.org/
Focus: Focused on providing trauma-informed care and education, this site helps individuals understand trauma recovery and offers resources to improve overall mental health.

8. National Institute of Mental Health (NIMH)
Website: https://www.nimh.nih.gov/
Focus: Provides comprehensive information on various mental health disorders, treatments, and research, offering resources for healing and self-awareness.

International Resources

1. Lifeline (Australia)
Phone Number: 13 11 14
Website: https://www.lifeline.org.au/
Focus: Provides 24/7 crisis support for those experiencing emotional distress or suicidal thoughts in Australia.

2. Samaritans (UK & Ireland)
Phone Number: 116 123
Website: https://www.samaritans.org/
Focus: Confidential support for anyone experiencing a personal crisis, providing emotional support and mental health guidance.

3. The Canadian Mental Health Association (CMHA)
Website: https://cmha.ca/
Focus: Offers mental health resources and services for Canadians, including self-care and trauma recovery programs. (Different numbers for different programs)Healing chapters

Notes...

Notes...